WILD FLORIDA

Secrets from Florida's Master Anglers

UNIVERSITY PRESS OF FLORIDA

Florida A&M University, Tallahassee
Florida Atlantic University, Boca Raton
Florida Gulf Coast University, Ft. Myers
Florida International University, Miami
Florida State University, Tallahassee
New College of Florida, Sarasota
University of Central Florida, Orlando
University of Florida, Gainesville
University of North Florida, Jacksonville
University of South Florida, Tampa
University of West Florida, Pensacola

Secrets from Florida's Master Anglers

Ron Presley

Foreword by M. Timothy O'Keefe
Artwork by Julie Sutton

University Press of Florida
Gainesville · Tallahassee · Tampa · Boca Raton
Pensacola · Orlando · Miami · Jacksonville · Ft. Myers · Sarasota

14 13 12 11 10 09   6 5 4 3 2 1

Library of Congress Cataloging-in-Publication Data
Presley, Ron.
Secrets from Florida's master anglers / Ron Presley; foreword by M. Timothy O'Keefe.
p. cm.—(Wild Florida)
Includes index.
ISBN 978-0-8130-3397-6 (alk. paper)
1. Saltwater fishing—Florida. 2. Fishers—Florida. I. Title.
SH483.P74 2009
799.16'0916348—dc22 2009018573

The University Press of Florida is the scholarly publishing agency for the State University System of Florida, comprising Florida A&M University, Florida Atlantic University, Florida Gulf Coast University, Florida International University, Florida State University, New College of Florida, University of Central Florida, University of Florida, University of North Florida, University of South Florida, and University of West Florida.

University Press of Florida
15 Northwest 15th Street
Gainesville, FL 32611-2079
http://www.upf.com

WILD FLORIDA
Edited by M. Timothy O'Keefe

Books in this series are written for the many people who visit and/or move to Florida to participate in our remarkable outdoors, an environment rich in birds, animals, and activities, many exclusive to this state. Books in the series will offer readers a variety of formats: Natural history guides, historical outdoor guides, guides to some of Florida's most popular pastimes and activities, and memoirs of outdoors folk and their unique lifestyles.

30 Eco-trips in Florida: The Best Nature Excursions (and How to Leave Only Your Footprnts), by Holly Ambrose (2005)

A Hiker's Guide to the Sunshine State, by Sandra Friend (2005)

Fishing Florida's Flats: A Guide to Bonefish, Tarpon, Permit, and Much More, by Jan S. Maizler (2007)

50 Great Walks in Florida, by Lucy Beebe Tobias (2008)

Hiking the Florida Trail: 1,100 Miles, 78 Days, Two Pairs of Boots, and One Heck of an Adventure, by Johnny Molloy (2008)

The Complete Florida Beach Guide, by Mary and Bill Burnham (2008)

The Saltwater Angler's Guide to Florida's Big Bend and Emerald Coast, by Tommy L. Thompson (2009)

Secrets from Florida's Master Anglers, by Ron Presley (2009)

To my wife Karen for unending support
and my grandson Robert, my best fishing buddy.

Contents

Foreword

Already one of the most-populous states, Florida still absorbs hundreds of thousands of new residents every year. So it may seem unlikely that truly wild places can remain anywhere in such a densely inhabited region. Fortunately, in spite of the tremendous influx of people wanting to enjoy the Sunshine State's warm climate and active outdoor lifestyle, significant sections of natural Florida still endure, including far more of our coastline than most residents or visitors ever realize.

The University Press of Florida in its broad-ranging series, *Wild Florida*, once again explores the state's coastal waters with *Secrets from Florida's Master Anglers* by Ron Presley. However, previous books have concentrated on angling for only a few species of gamefish (*Fishing Florida's Flats: A Guide to Bonefish, Tarpon, Permit, and Much More* by Jan S. Maizler) or limited regions (*The Saltwater Angler's Guide to Florida's Big Bend and Emerald Coast* by Tommy Thompson).

Ron Presley writes with a much broader approach including basics for overall tackle selection, techniques for fishing different baits, and shortening your angling learning curve with the help of a good guide. A professional guide himself, Ron Presley knows what he is talking about. But he also recognizes that he doesn't know it all, which is why his book draws on the expertise of numerous other guides—and the reason the book is called *Secrets from Florida's Master Anglers*. This makes the book truly a one-of-a-kind for Florida fishing. But I defer to Frank Sargeant (very longtime friend), one of Florida's premier outdoor writers and editors to testify to the title's accuracy in the Preface that follows.

Instead, I want to point out why so many books in the *Wild Florida* series have explored Florida's recreational fishing opportunities. Without question angling is one of Florida's most popular outdoor activities. According to the Florida Fish and Wildlife Conservation Commission, Florida attracts more anglers than any other state in the country, with an average of 46.3 million days of fishing annually including residents and non-residents.

In 2007, the U.S. Census Bureau released the eleventh in a series of surveys that have been conducted every five years since 1955. In the "National Survey of Fishing, Hunting, and Wildlife-Associated Recreation," Florida once again topped the nation in every conceivable category related to fishing. Specifically, they are:

- Resident Anglers (2.8 million vs. #2 Texas with 2.5 million).
- Angler Expenditures in State ($4.4 billion vs. #2 Texas with $3.4 billion). By comparison, the 1991–92 expenditures was $1.3 billion.
- Angler supported jobs (75,068 vs. #2 Texas with 59,938).
- State and local taxes generated by sportfishing ($440 million vs. #2 Texas with $392 million).
- Non-resident (tourists) anglers (885,000 vs. #2 North Carolina 395,000).
- Non-resident expenditures ($1.0 billion vs. #2 Wisconsin $0.6 billion).
- Fishing days per angler: 17.2 days annually.

Anglers are devoted to their sport, averaging 17.2 days annually for a total of 46.3 million fishing days. The individual participation may not seem significant but it requires far more effort to arrange a full day of fishing away from home versus a few hours on the local tennis court.

Interestingly, in Florida, saltwater anglers (resident and non-resident) outnumber freshwater fisherman 2 million vs. 1.4 million, and most out-of-state anglers visit to test their skills in the coastal waters.

This is why Ron Presley's *Secrets from Florida's Master Anglers* is a welcome and much-needed addition to *Wild Florida*. Now, go fish!

M. Timothy O'Keefe
Series Editor

Preface

Getting started in saltwater angling is a challenge for anyone new to coastal waters, but this book can make it far easier. Author Ron Presley, himself a guide, has tapped the expertise of his friends and associates, all of them seasoned fishing guides, to cover every aspect of what it takes to locate and catch all the best-known coastal species.

The book begins with tackle selection. The right gear makes a huge difference in success or failure. Most anglers coming to saltwater for the first time burden themselves with gear that's far too heavy, but Presley and his friends guide you through the selection process to the tackle that's just right for handling the species you most want to catch.

There's a chapter that covers tying all the necessary knots for building a good leader, tying on lures, creating a double line, and lots more. And there's an up-to-the-minute discussion of using conventional or J-hooks versus more environmentally conscious circle hooks.

Casting can be a big part of success in some venues, and Ron's book gives lots of tips on how to make long, accurate casts under a variety of conditions. There's a chapter on wade-fishing and fishing from boats, the shore, bridges, piers—anywhere there might be a fish nearby.

Separate chapters cover catching and using live bait—with tips on keeping the bait lively—and artificial-lure selection and use.

From metal spoons to plastic shrimp, many of the latest lures are reviewed.

And when you hook that trophy, you'll want to know how to get it to the boat. There's a chapter on fighting fish, setting the drag right, and using the power of the rod to beat big fish on modest tackle, every time. Just as important in this day of catch and release, there's a section on handling fish so that they'll survive to fight another day.

There's also a chapter on good manners on the water—I wish every angler could read it. As more and more people enjoy our coastal waters each year, there are more frequent conflicts over anglers getting too close to each other. Learning the basic rules of sharing the water is important to all of us these days.

For those a bit bewildered by the need for all the rules and regulations on coastal fishing, there's a chapter explaining some of the philosophy behind them; learning the basics of conservation and fishery management can make all of us better citizen-anglers.

And of course Ron devotes a couple of chapters to fishing with guides—tips on finding and hiring a good guide, what the guides can do for you and what they can't. And the grand finale is a chapter thumbnailing all the guides who shared their expertise in this book. In this final chapter, all the guides share their best secret for fishing success.

Overall, this is a great guidebook for anyone interested in getting started in saltwater fishing, and even those who have been at it for years can't help but learn plenty from its pages.

Frank Sargeant

Acknowledgments

This book is an inquiry into the minds of twenty Florida master anglers. Intended for fishermen and fisherwomen of all skill levels, it shares numerous tips and suggestions on becoming a better angler. The information obtained from the master anglers is a mix of philosophy related to the fishery resource, as well as authoritative tips for applying successful fishing techniques. The philosophies have been developed by years of experience on the water and the recurring observations of an ecosystem that has changed greatly over the last few decades. The applications of know-how and techniques are hard-earned secrets, developed by years of professional fishing experience.

From tying proper knots, to landing the big one, this book touches all aspects of inshore light-tackle fishing in Florida, with a hint of the nearshore possibilities as well. Its pages reveal fishing techniques that can be applied around the world. Florida's master anglers are strong advocates of conservation and protection of the fishery resource, and that philosophy is well represented in the book. Anecdotal entries scattered throughout connect the reader in a personal way to the participating master anglers.

The book should be read with the intent of discovering practical information in unlikely places, as the guides respond to various elements of saltwater fishing. It will engage you in an educational process that makes you a better angler. The book also guides the reader toward developing a mutual respect for other anglers and the fishing environment itself.

I gratefully acknowledge the twenty fishing guides who willingly contributed to the pages of this book. Their love for the sport and concern for the resource speaks volumes for their character. They are all identified specifically in the last chapter, along with their contact information.

A special note of gratitude goes to my daughter, Karol Woody, for her proofreading, editing, and general support of the project.

Finally, I extend my sincere thanks to the unnamed reviewers of the manuscript for their thoughtful criticism and suggested revisions that added greatly to the finished product.

A Knowledge Base for Angling

What Every Angler Should Know

God may be the master of the universe, but professional anglers are the masters of the water. The term "master" refers to someone who is an authority in a specific art or discipline. When applied to Florida's master anglers, the term means they are qualified to teach others the knowledge and skills that they have developed over many years of experience. From shallow-water flats to deep ocean currents, professional fishing guides are more capable of helping you improve your saltwater fishing success than any other group of people on earth. So, if you want to learn from the masters, read on and discover how Florida's master anglers can improve your fishing success by sharing their hard-earned secrets with you.

Once you acquire the knowledge that these master anglers have to offer, you will know a lot more about fishing—and catching too. Whether you apply those skills as your ancestors did, to gather food for the table, or use them like many modern-day anglers, as a way to relax and enjoy the great outdoors through catch-and-release fishing, your overall fishing experience will improve immensely—and the pleasure in your hobby will likewise increase.

Acquiring Knowledge

An individual's fishing ability can be built either through personal experience or by learning from others who have studied the sport. Either way, your ability will improve as you accumulate the knowledge and skills to be a better angler. The knowledge you develop is not a single element to be included in your tackle box but an accumulation of what you can learn about the sport. Skills and techniques are developed as you practice your new avocation. The two go together like a lock and a key. Each has a role to play, but neither is complete without the other. When used together, their value increases exponentially. Building a bridge between angling knowledge and fishing skills or techniques is what this book is all about.

Capt. Bouncer Smith, a charter captain on Florida's East Coast, suggests that you begin your quest for fishing knowledge with a simple appreciation and understanding of the sport. He says, "First you must understand the sport of fishing. I define the sport of fishing as the best use of time shared with yourself, or better yet, with good friends or family. It's enjoying nature in all its glory, whether it's birds, wildlife, clouds, mountains, rushing water, quiet ponds, or just peace and quiet. Then you can add the suspense of fishing action."

Anglers who wish to have success need to have some knowledge about a fish's favorite foods, how fish react to the weather and sea-

Fishing is about spending quality time with good friends or family.

sons, the temperature at which different species of fish are comfortable, knowing what knots to tie, whether to use a monofilament or fluorocarbon leader, or which rod and reel to use for a certain species of fish. How much you know and how you apply that knowledge will directly affect your fishing success.

Just remember, you are not going to obtain all fishing knowledge in one day or one year or even a lifetime. It's a continuous effort made over time that helps you add to your knowledge base. Capt. Jim Savaglio, of Valrico, Florida, says, "I believe fishing success requires anglers to continuously increase their knowledge. Think about it. Every time you go fishing, you try to figure out how you can get just one more fish to the boat, if you only had a little more knowledge."

Keeping in mind that these and other fishing tips will be covered in more detail later in the book, let's consider a few ideas that some of Florida's master anglers think you should include in your knowledge base.

Equipment

Capt. Blair Wiggins, host of the popular TV fishing show *Addictive Fishing,* says that, foremost, anglers need to be familiar with their equipment.

Captain Smith agrees. He says, "The first thing an angler needs to know is how to use his equipment—how to set the drag, cast the reel, and match the tackle to the targeted fish."

In addition to understanding how the tackle functions, fishermen should know the type of tackle and equipment to use for different applications. Capt. Rick Burns, who fishes near Homosassa, advises, "Don't head out with tackle that's too heavy to cast if you plan to throw artificial lures all day. On the other hand, you won't have much success if you take casting rods to a trolling party." Undersize rods and oversize fish do not add up to success—only to disappointment.

In addition to the rod and reel, anglers should be familiar with the utility and variety of fishing line. Capt. Robert McCue, who's as well known as a conservationist as he is as a guide, says that what seems like a simple decision—picking a line—depends on the type of fishing you do. McCue uses braided line on everything these days, with few exceptions. Recognizing the exceptions is an important part of your knowledge base and will be discussed further in Chapter 3.

Knowledge of your equipment and how to use it is something you can develop when you are not fishing—say on those days when it's too windy or rainy to fish. When poor weather keeps you inside, dedicate some time to improving your knowledge base and skill level—tying knots, for example—so you will be more efficient and successful the next time you do go fishing.

Captain McCue often uses an old saying from his days in the Marine Corps: "The more we prepare in peace, the less we bleed in war." He relates these words to the large amount of down time often associated with recreational angling and boating. When equipment isn't used, it sometimes develops problems. "Keeping your boat and

Being familiar with your equipment is the first step to fishing success. Match your rods, reels, and lines to your targeted fish.

fishing gear in top shape reduces the likelihood of having to spend time fixing problems when on the water."

Weather

Knowing how to read the weather is an extremely important element of your fishing-knowledge base. In my own experience as a fishing guide I can remember many times when it would have been better to just stay at home, turn up the heat, and read a fishing magazine. Guides, however, cater to clients who may have only one day to fish during their visit to an area—and guides have to roll with the

Weather can make or break your fishing trip. Learn how to stay on top of it.

punches. And when the conditions are bad, it's even more important to be able to draw upon a well of knowledge and instincts to find the fish. The weather can have a major impact on both what you fish for and where you fish.

Solunar Tables, Tides, and the Moon

Expert anglers consider knowledge of the tides an important element of fishing success. Capt. Rick Grassett, a prominent fishing guide in southwestern Florida, says that an understanding of tides and how they affect fishing lets the angler know the best time to fish. For many anglers the best time to go fishing is when you can, but in reality, if you want your trip to be productive you should consult the tide tables and plan your trip accordingly.

Closely related to tide tables, solunar tables identify four periods during each day when fish are said to be more active and feeding.

The tables are based on the relationship of the sun (sol) and moon (lunar) to each other and how they affect the tides. Chapter 5 will offer a more in-depth presentation of the tides and the associated moon phases.

Water Temperature

Fish are cold-blooded animals, so their body temperatures are always the same as the temperature of the water around them. Water temperature and a fish's comfort level are other factors anglers need to consider. The reason is fairly simple. If you get too hot you are likely to move indoors to an air-conditioned environment to reestablish your level of comfort. If you are too cold you'll seek warmth. Fish aren't much different.

Since water temperatures vary with the seasons and water depths, your success in finding a particular species of fish may depend on knowing what range of temperatures they prefer and where to find areas where that range is obtained. Oftentimes, if you find the right water temperature, you also find your targeted fish.

Fishing Knots

Although not the most exciting element of fishing, knot tying is one of the basic elements you'll need to master in order to have fishing success. I can't think of anything worse than hooking a nice fish and fighting it for a period of time only to have it pull off because the knot failed. It's easy to spot the remains of a bad knot: The tag end will look like a squiggly little pig tail—sure evidence that the line did not break and that the knot just pulled out.

Most angling situations do not require many fishing knots; a few will handle most applications. In the end, it's not how many knots you know, but how well you tie them.

Further information on when and where to use different knots will be discussed throughout the chapters of this book.

Fishing History

History represents an accumulation of knowledge. As far as fishing is concerned, your personal history will become a part of the knowledge base that tells you where the fish were last time, where the fish were last year at this time under similar weather conditions, or maybe where the bait was on your last trip or even last year.

Many master anglers employ a log to record such data and then use the log for planning their future fishing expeditions. Some anglers simply make notes on their calendar or hand write daily trip information into a notebook. Other fishermen use computers and one of many software applications available that allow data to be logged and manipulated for future use. Information on developing and using logbooks will be given in Chapter 5.

Making the Link between Knowledge and Skill

In the business world, it's well known that knowledge is one of the most important resources a company can have. Similarly, on the fishing scene, knowledge will certainly separate the expert angler from the novice. Good anglers devote themselves to obtaining more information in the pursuit of their fishing success. If you are a tournament angler, fishing is a competitive sport and most tournament fishermen will tell you that knowing more than your competitors can give you the edge you need to win. If you are not a competitive fisherman, and this includes most anglers, knowledge will still give you a competitive advantage over the fish.

Developing the link between acquiring fishing knowledge and developing fishing skills and techniques is the key to greater fishing success. Capt. Dave Sutton sums up the notion of acquiring fishing knowledge when he says, "Fishing is not just a sport; it is a passion. Treat it like one—everyday!" Your passion will lead you to acquire knowledge, and when coupled with appropriate skills, your fishing success will improve.

Recreational fishing, as the name implies, is a therapeutic activity for most anglers. To be truly therapeutic, fishing should actively involve anglers in the process of both fishing and catching. Although we all claim that it's nice just being out there, in reality, fishing is more therapeutic when a whole lot of catchin' goes along with the fishin.' It just makes good sense to invest in the knowledge now and reap the rewards on your next fishing trip, as well as all those trips to come in the future.

The remainder of this book is aimed at expanding your knowledge base and improving your fishing achievements.

Last Cast

Given the importance of acquiring your own personal store of knowledge to fishing success, don't forget to just enjoy the experience for what it's really worth. A friend of mine, Capt. Bob Zales, ends all his e-mails with a quote that hangs on the wall of a ladies clothing store in Islamorada, Florida. The quote states, "The charm of fishing is that, it is the pursuit of what is elusive, but attainable; a perpetual series of occasions for hope."

2

Captain's Choice

Selecting Your Rod and Reel

As the sun came out from behind the clouds, a huge, dark silhouette, long as a log, appeared on the port side of the boat. My fishing partner yelled, "Nice cobia at one o'clock!" He reached for a rod and made a cast to the cruising fish. It immediately made a descent to follow the chartreuse jig as it fell toward the ocean floor. *Bam!* The fish was hooked, and my friend was nearly overpowered by the big cobia he had hooked on a medium-weight inshore rod that just happened to be the closest rod available. He managed to land the 40-pound cobia, but only after a time-consuming fight and after opportunities to catch other fish were lost. This experience is a prime example of why it is so important to choose the right rod for the fish that you intend to catch and then match it up with the right reel and line.

Choosing a Rod

Most inshore guides recommend a medium-weight rod for typical flats-fishing applications. You can successfully land trout, redfish, and snook in open water with a medium-action rod using 8- to 10-pound-test line and a 15- to 20-pound monofilament or fluorocarbon leader.

There are, however, times when you will want to choose a different outfit. If you are fishing for oversize redfish or large snook around docks or other structure, you will have to beef up the rod so it has more backbone. You'll also need the reel spooled with heavier line and leader.

"Your rod purchase should be dictated by your fishing conditions," says Capt. Dave Sutton, who began guiding in Rhode Island before moving to Florida. "If you fish heavy cover, such as the mangroves or docks for snook, you will need a medium-to-heavy rod and at least 20-pound test. But on the flats, a medium rod and 10-pound test will do just fine."

Almost 100 percent of the rods used by professional anglers are one-piece rods, which provide more strength and give the angler more sensitivity to what's going on at the other end of the line than do rods of two or more pieces. One reason for *not* choosing a one-piece rod would be if you are traveling and need to break the rod down for packing convenience.

Your choice of rods will be one of the most important decisions you make, and it will impact your angling success more than you might think. Captain Sutton says, "Buy a good one right off the bat. It is much cheaper to own a good rig than to buy several of the cheaper ones before you go to a good outfit. Successful anglers will eventually own the good stuff." The fishing rod becomes an extension of the angler and his fishing strategy. Unfortunately, there is not a single rod on the market that will fill the bill for all the types of fishing. Two or three rods, however, will likely fulfill the needs of most anglers. In choosing that perfect rod you will consider strength or action, taper, material, and length.

Rod Length

When it comes time to choose a rod, make your selection based on the type of fish you target and the environment in which you fish. The question of length may be the easiest choice of all in your selection of a rod.

If you fish mostly in tight restricted areas, such as narrow, mangrove-lined cuts or channels, you will want to choose a relatively short rod. Rods for this type of fishing are designed for casting accuracy and may be as much as a foot shorter than the average 7-foot rods used on the flats. Offshore anglers who want to turn the heads of large fish away from the bottom and retrieve fish from bottom lairs, also choose short powerful rods. Common rods for this non-casting application range from 6-foot to 6-foot 6-inches in length. These rods are not only shorter than rods made for casting but also larger in diameter, to provide the needed strength in this application.

Long rods are used in the open waters of a bay or river. Much of Florida is characterized by this type of open-water fishing. Long rods are also used when the angler wants to make a long cast or throw a lighter lure or bait. Longer rods give the angler more distance, plus they take some of the stress off the line and place it on the rod when fighting a fish. For day-to-day fishing on open waters, a rod length of seven feet or more is commonly used by Florida's master anglers.

Capt. Pat Dineen, who guides out of Shalimar, Florida, likes a 7-foot fast-action 8- to 15-pound rod manufactured by G. Loomis, and he uses it for reds and general inshore light-tackle fishing.

Captain Pat says, "Buy something you will be happy with after you become an experienced angler, otherwise you will end up buying another outfit when you realize the lower-value rod just doesn't perform like you want it to."

Capt. Blair Wiggins, who grew up in Florida, actually got to participate in the development of the rod he uses most. He teamed up with Wright & McGill Company in the development of a 7-foot 9-inch model that he uses for redfish, sea trout, snook, permit, tarpon to 90 pounds, mangrove snapper, stripers, flounder, jacks, bluefish, cobia, and even largemouth bass. The rod is medium-action, with a carbon Kevlar wrap over high-modulus graphite. He says, "This wrap enables me to target a wide variety of fish without having to change rods all the time. It also cuts down on having a whole slew of rods in my collection."

The idea of not having to change rods often also appeals to Capt. Dave Sutton, who chooses a medium-action 7-foot rod with a soft tip. This rod enables him to cast soft plastics to snook and redfish, while maintaining the ability to effectively work a surface rig such as a Rapala Skitter-Walk.

Opting for a longer rod, Capt. Robert McCue prefers an 8-foot fast-action rod. "The lower one-third of the rod is very stiff, but the tip is light," he says. This type of rod is commonly referred to as a live-bait rod. The length, the fast action, and the light tip provide optimum casting distance for live bait. "The lower one-third of this rod is stiff as a broom stick. It is this lowest section and the third above that provide the strength to fight big fish on light tackle. The overall length and design allows for high-pressure stopping power as the rod acts like a whip. I do not think there is a species of fish swimming the waters of Florida that these type rods will not land."

He says people often question the lightness and action of the rods and whether they will land really big fish. "It's all about the dynamics and physics," he says, "and this rod is very effective in catching hard-fighting, fast, and bullish flats fish. The extra length provides more casting distance, which means I can stay farther away from wary, pressured, spooky fish in gin-clear water and still make effective presentations." Captain McCue uses this versatile rod for snook, redfish, trout, jacks, small to mid-size kings, juvenile tarpon, pompano, and bluefish.

Capt. Rick Burns fishes out of Homosassa where he targets redfish, trout, snook, Spanish mackerel, small shark, bluefish, and other saltwater species with his favorite 7-foot 6-inch graphite rod. He also insists on a one-piece rod. In fact, he says, "If it's two pieces, glue it." Because he casts a lot of plugs, he likes shorter-than-average cork handles for more maneuverability. His choice of rod would contain nine line guides made from titanium or silicon carbide. The nine guides allow the mainline to follow the curve of the rod under the load of a heavy fish. These quality line guides decrease friction between the line and the guides, and promote maximum casting distance when the rod is matched with a proper reel and line.

Rod Action

Once you have determined the type and general size of the fish you want to target, you can easily choose a rod with the appropriate action. A rod's action is what determines its lifting power or strength. Rods come in several standard actions that include ultra-light, light, medium, medium-heavy, heavy, and extra-heavy.

The best place to start in choosing a rod is to consider the size of the fish you are likely to catch and the size of the line you will need to bring them in. Most rods will be marked between the reel seat and the first guide with the line sizes that can best be used with the rod. For example you might read "XTR79MS 7' Med Act 1/8-1/2 Lure wt. 4-12 lb. Line." The first set of letters and numbers is simply the manufacturer's model number. The remaining information gives the length of the rod, the action of the rod, the size of lure the rod is designed to cast, and the weight of the line to be used on a matching reel.

Captain Dineen uses a light-action 7-foot rod for most applications but reminds anglers that there is not one rod that fills all needs. He says, "I like light-action rods for lure fishing. They load well and cast a lure a long way accurately. For live-bait fishing, particularly free-lining live baits, I prefer a medium-action; the bait doesn't get thrown off the hook as easily on the cast."

Rod Taper

Rods come with yet another choice, taper. Taper controls the way the rod flexes under pressure and is a part of the overall action of the rod. Some rods will have the taper marked on the blank near the reel seat with the other information, but many manufactures include it in their action classification.

Taper is designated as extra-fast, fast, medium-fast, medium, and slow. A fast-taper rod is one that tapers quickly into a stronger part of the blank. Its arc under the pressure of a fish will bend only about the first one-third of the rod. The result is a sensitive tip for feeling a subtle strike, while at the same time, providing a strong backbone for hook-setting and for fighting brawny fish.

The "taper" of a fishing rod describes the flex of the rod under pressure. A fast-taper rod will bend only at the top one-third of the rod.

Capt. Tom Van Horn, who guides the Indian River Lagoon, likes to use the Evolution medium-action rod with a fast taper. He says, "The fast taper loads nicely when casting, adding an additional 15 percent more distance to your cast with braided line, and the solid graphite provides for better sensitivity."

A slow-taper rod will bend into the stronger part of the blank over a greater distance and lends itself to more of a C shape when fighting a fish. There is not as much backbone in the slow-taper rod. The general action of any rod will depend on both the weight and the taper, and takes into account the size of a fish the rod can handle.

Capt. Ed "Jazz" Jazwierski, who grew up fishing the Midwest, favors medium-fast to fast taper rods for the hookset. "I feel the more bend your rod has the further you need to pull it back to set the hook. That extra foot or two may be time enough for the fish to feel the tension and spit out the bait before you have a chance to set the hook."

Fishing with different tapers is the best way to determine the rod you like best. Either fishing with a guide and using his rods or borrowing a rod from a friend is a good way to start your search. In the end it's all about how the fishing rod feels and performs in the type of fishing that you do most.

Rod Material

Early rods were made from tree limbs or bamboo. The main purpose of these early-day rods was to cast the bait further from the shore of a river or lake. Bamboo or cane poles are still used by shore-bound anglers to extend the reach of their angling pursuits. Most modern-day rods, however, are made from fiberglass or graphite, and they are engineered to accept a reel spooled with several hundred yards of fishing line.

Fiberglass rods are good choices for beginning anglers and children, because these rods are relatively inexpensive and withstand a lot of abuse. Fiberglass rods require little maintenance and will give years of service.

Graphite rods have become the choice of most experienced anglers, because they are lighter and stronger than rods made from other materials. Graphite rods are made by laminating carbon fibers into a hollow rod blank using hi-tech resins and modern technology. There are many variations in the quality of graphite rods, and the quality and performance will be reflected in the price.

Capt. Chris Myers is owner-operator of Florida Fishing Lessons, a light-tackle charter and fishing-instruction service. He mostly fishes the Mosquito Lagoon and the Indian River, chasing redfish, tarpon, trout, snook and jacks. His choice of rod for day-to-day duty on all these fish is a 7-foot 6-inch graphite rod with a medium action.

For Captain Myers, "A light-action rod often does not have enough backbone to set the hook in some larger fish. A stiff rod will not cast as accurately. The medium is a good blend." He matches this rod with a 2500 size reel because it is very light and holds plenty of line for the fish he targets.

In contrast to Captain Myers's choice of targeted fish and rod selection, Capt. Keith Kalbfleisch likes to slow-troll for tarpon and kings in the nearshore Atlantic Ocean, mostly out of Cape Canaveral. He chooses a 6-foot-long medium-action boat rod with a fast taper. This rod is a combination of fiberglass and graphite that most companies call kingfish or live-bait rods. "I want a soft tip on the rod that will flex when the boat moves so that my bait stays alive. However, I still need a rod with some backbone to fight a big fish." He will match the rod with a revolving spool reel, which can hold at least 400 yards of 30-pound braided line over a backing of 100 yards of 20-pound mono. "This gives me a huge amount of line to manage a big fish, yet it can be done on a smaller reel than we previously used—it's the magic of braid!"

Capt. Rick Burns prefers intermediate modulus-graphite-composite rods because of their light weight, high sensitivity, and balance for added fish-fighting power. An IM6 or IM7 works well for him. "These rods are light but strong and will not wear you out when casting all day," he says. When these lightweight graphite rods are matched with lightweight reels, the reduced stress and fatigue associated with a daylong casting adventure makes them well worth the investment. These rods will give years of service, when maintained regularly.

Rod Maintenance

Even the highest-quality rods will require periodic cleaning and maintenance to ensure performance. The cleaning process is simple, but given the harsh saltwater environment they are exposed to, it is not something you want to forget. The parts of the rod vulnerable to saltwater are the line guides, or eyes, so be sure to clean them well. You should also check the eyes for nicks and abrasions that might damage your line. Simply pull an old pair of pantyhose through each guide—the pantyhose will hang up on the nicks and abrasions—and you will quickly discover any problems you may have.

After using your rods in saltwater, spray them up and down with fresh water from a garden hose, being sure to spray the guides on both the top and bottom sides. Apply a light soapy solution first to help dissolve the salt crystals before rinsing the rods. It helps to use a soft brush to fully clean the guides from the salty residue. It is not necessary to do this every time, but it certainly wouldn't hurt.

If your reels are still attached, as they usually are, be careful not to hit them with the full force of the water pressure. Full pressure is fine on the rod, but you do not want to force water into the interior of the reel. Wipe down and dry the rod with a soft cloth to remove excess water.

Some master anglers apply a light coat of furniture polish at this point to help retain the rich finish that characterizes most modern rods. After a minute or two, simply buff the rod with a clean cloth and it will produce the rich luster and shine of a newly purchased rod. Finally, spray the rod with a water dispersant such as Reel Magic to further protect it from the elements. If your reel is still attached, it can be sprayed too, for additional protection.

Take a look at table 1, and follow the recommendations of Florida master anglers to help you match a rod-and-reel combination to a specific game fish.

Table 1. Rod and Spinning-Reel Selection

Fish	Rod	Reel Size
Redfish 0–20 lbs	7 to 8 ft. Lt or Med Action	2500 to 4000
Redfish 20 plus lbs	7 ft. Med/Hvy or Hvy	4000 to 5000
Sea Trout	7 to 8 ft. Lt or Med Action	2500
Snook 0–20 lbs	7 ft. Lt or Med Action	4000
Snook 20 plus lbs	7 ft. Med/Hvy or Hvy	5000
Tarpon 0–20 lbs	7 ft. Lt. or Med Action	4000
Tarpon 20–40 lbs	7 ft. Med/Hvy or Hvy	5000
Tarpon 40–100 lbs	7 ft. Hvy or X-HVY	6000
Tarpon 100 plus lbs	X-Hvy	8000

Note: The rod material is left to the individual angler's budget and preference. Rod actions and reel sizes are minimums; heavier equipment will bring the fish to the boat quicker and possibly enhance a live release.

Reel Selection

Given the numerous choices available on the market today, the matching of a reel to go with your newly selected rod is not as complicated as you might think. There are several general characteristics that you will want to consider when choosing a reel to match your choice of rod.

Size of Targeted Fish

One of the first considerations in reel choice is the size of the fish you intend to target. The larger the fish, the larger the reel you need. Of course, the smaller the fish, the smaller the reel you will need. But I've noticed that more anglers *oversize* their reels than *undersize* them, especially the novice anglers who purchase that first rod and reel with only one thought in mind—catching a really big one. Would-be anglers, however, would be wise to base their choice of reel on the average fish—the fish they're most likely to catch the most—than on the dream of catching the big one.

Most master anglers will tell you from their own fishing experiences that they have tended to downsize their reels as new materials and technology have made fishing tackle stronger, lighter, and more dependable. Today's smaller reels will perform better than some of the larger reels of the past. Even if you only want to catch the big ones, you may not need as large a reel as you first thought.

The other important consideration related to the size of the fish is the line capacity of your reel. Redfish, for example, can make long hard runs that quickly deplete the line on a smaller reel. You certainly do not want to get spooled by a big red, so be sure your reel will hold a sufficient amount of line to handle the size and characteristics of the fish you expect to catch.

Method of Fishing

Your method of fishing will be your next important consideration. If you get your fishing enjoyment from casting artificial lures, you will make hundreds of casts in a day of fishing. If this is how you like to fish, then you should be thinking about the weight of the reel (and rod). Remember, today's reels are engineered better with lighter weight materials. The performance of any given size reel is better than reels of comparable size from years gone by.

If you like to bait up, cast out, and wait for the fish to come to you, then the weight of the reel is not as important, because you are not carrying it around and casting it all day. In this case it makes sense to use a larger rod and reel that will allow you to target various sizes of fish and land them with equal levels of success.

Gear Ratio

Reels come with various gear ratios, which is simply the number of times the line spool turns for each turn of the handle. My Shimano 2500, for example, has a gear ratio of 6.0:1. This means every time I crank the handle one turn, the spool turns six times. This is a relatively fast ratio and will put line back on the spool in a hurry, which is especially useful when a hooked fish swims directly toward you and you need to retrieve the slack line quickly and efficiently.

If you need a slower retrieve and more cranking power, you would want to select a reel with a lower ratio. Regardless of the gear ratio, light-tackle reels are not made to winch the fish to the boat; it's the angler's responsibility to use the rod, in combination with the reel, to land the fish. Proper techniques of fighting fish with any reel will be presented in Chapter 8.

Ball Bearings

The number and quality of ball bearings in a reel will determine how smoothly it operates. When selecting a reel, turn the handle and listen for noise and feel for vibration. Do this with several different reels, and you will see the difference quality ball bearings make. Fishing in a saltwater environment takes a toll on all metal equipment, and good reels are made of metal components. Quality bearings are an investment well worth making if you want to get years of service from your reel. My Shimano 2500 has four ball bearings and one roller bearing, a combination that provides a smooth non-vibrating retrieve for efficient replacement of the line on the spool. As you would expect, the more ball bearings the higher the cost, so buy the highest-quality reel your budget will allow.

There is no substitute for going to your favorite fishing-supply stores and trying out various models before buying. As a side note, don't forget to include your local tackle shops and marinas when shopping. They often have competitive prices, but they also offer a lot more service and other fishing information than the big discount stores. When you do make the comparison between various reels first hand, you will discover for yourself the difference the number of ball bearings in the reel makes in its operation.

Drag

The drag is also an important part of the reel. This is another area where uneducated anglers tend to miss the point. Most novice anglers set the drag too tight. The purpose of the drag is to take the pressure of a big fish off the reel and let it be applied to the rod. Remember, modern rods and reels are made very well. Capt. Blair Wiggins says, "Given the design of today's rods, all you have to remember about the reel is that the handle on the reel is made only to wind line back onto the spool. It's not a winch."

The quality of the drag system will show when it's pushed to the limit—that is, when you're battling a great fish. The idea of the drag is to pay out line to the fish in a smooth even manner at a desired setting. Cheaper reels usually have cheaper drags, and the precision of the system does not allow the line to come off the spool freely. If the line leaves the spool in a jerky and erratic manner, the uneven pressure can cause your line to break. In fact, many line breaks are caused by a snap of a line going from slack to tight rather than from a steady straight pull from a fish. An improperly functioning drag can allow slack that can lead to a lost fish.

Captain Jazz says, "When shopping for a reel, the first thing I look at is the drag system, and I check to see if the line pays out smoothly. Saltwater fish such as snook, redfish, and tarpon will always test your drag system with powerful runs. Your drag should pay out smoothly, or something bad is going to happen. You could lose the fish, break the line, lose a lure, or even break the rod."

In some way, though, your choice of reel will come down to budget. With that in mind, select a reel that has a smooth-working and easily adjustable drag on the highest quality reel that you can afford.

Chapter 8 will explain the relationship of drag settings with fighting and landing fish. The chapter will also give instruction on how to properly set the drag to match your fishing conditions. One thing you never do is crank against the drag. Mono and fluorocarbon line will twist, weaken, and lose performance if the angler turns the crank on a spinning reel while the drag is screaming.

Type of Reel

Once you have decided on the size of the reel, the next choice is what kind of a reel you need. The two reels used most often by Florida's master anglers are spinning and bait-casting reels. There are other types of reels, but we'll consider only these two because of their popularity among professional fishermen. Fly fishing is a whole other ballgame and considered beyond the scope of this book, but there are plenty of good references available for those who want to learn more.

Spinning Reels

Spinning reels are by far the most-popular reels employed by Florida's master anglers. Spinning reels serve up unlimited versatility by providing ease of use, great casting distance, and the ability to cast lightweight lures and live baits. Spinning reels can be used successfully on most species of fish in Florida.

On a spinning reel, the spool that holds the line remains fixed, while the line is pulled off in a spiraling motion by the weight of the terminal tackle. Long accurate casts can be made in this near frictionless environment, and long casts are sometimes needed to catch larger fish. Master flats anglers consistently comment that the larger fish are more cautious than smaller fish and often found farther from the boat.

With a spinning reel, the line is released by opening the bail, a wire device used to control when the line comes off and when the line is placed back on the spool. In the open position the angler can make a cast, followed by closing the bail to retrieve the line. Sometimes referred to as the pick up, the bail will pick up the line when in the closed position and wind the line back onto the spool. The bail is opened by hand for the cast and can be closed by turning the crank. However, most master anglers advise other fishermen to develop the habit of closing the bail by hand. More on this important technique of fishing will be given in the discussion on proper casting techniques in Chapter 4.

It is not unusual to visit a fishing location and see anglers holding a spinning rod and reel with the reel above the rod. If you observe them closely you will see that they have to wind backward to retrieve the line. Spinning reels are designed to suspend below the rod and be cast with the right hand, for a right-handed person. The line is retrieved by winding the handle with the left hand. Just the oppo-

Handles on spinning reels can be affixed to either side to accommodate right- or left-handed users. The reel on the right is rigged for a left-hander.

site is true for a southpaw. Most spinning reels come with reversible handles for easy adaptation to right- or left-handed users.

Spinning reels come with either front or back adjustable drags. The most popular type are the front-adjusting models that have a knob on the front of the line spool. The angler can tighten the drag by turning the adjusting knob clockwise and loosen it by turning it counter clockwise. The actual setting will depend on the size of the line you are using, the fish you are targeting, and the type of fishing you are doing.

To release the line from a spinning reel, the angler opens the bail while holding the line against the rod with his forefinger. A cast is made by releasing the line on the forward thrust of the rod. Great accuracy and long casts can be made with a properly matched spinning rod and reel.

Captain Van Horn has always been one to choose a middle-of-the-road reel that is durable, while still providing good value. He finds those characteristics in the Daiwa Exceller reels, "I use basically the same rods and select a 2500 size reel for jigging for smaller fish, the 3500 when casting larger plugs and spoons, and the 4500 size when targeting larger fish." He prefers braided line and attempts to land the fish as quickly as possible to reduce stress and minimize mortality of released fish.

Like many other master anglers, Captain McCue uses small reels that fit his requirements for fishing. He uses the Daiwa SS 1300 and matches it with the 8-foot fast-action rod. He says he often gets questioned by people on the ability of this combination to do the job with feisty fish. "I have been using these reels on my charters for nearly seventeen years. They are small, light, and designed for long casting. They are tough as nails and perfect for charter fishing with high-end tackle. I am aware of all the technology that has come about over the years with light spinning reels, but I will not change." These tough little reels hold about 160 yards of 14-pound Fireline, and according to Captain McCue, that's all you need. "In reality, most fish will not run more than fifty yards. I have been spooled, but it's rare." The 1300 is light, so holding and casting it all day is effortless. These reels were taken off the market a few years back, but then Daiwa started making them again, and they are now readily available to anglers.

If our master anglers are not using spinning reels, their next choice is the baitcasting reel. Don't think that one is better than the other; it just depends on how you are fishing and what you are fishing for.

Baitcasting Reels

Unlike spinning reels, baitcasting reels use a revolving spool to hold the line. The outgoing line is controlled by pressure of the angler's thumb on the spool. They are a little harder to master, because when a cast is made and the spool is revolving, it is possible for the speed of the spool to overrun the line and cause a backlash when a cast is made.

Anglers who fish around docks and other structure prefer baitcasters because these reels work better with the heavier line that is required for abrasion resistance. The biggest need for abrasion resistance comes when fishing around structure that the fish can use to cut you off. Baitcasters are often the reel of choice among bass anglers, but are also used in many applications on the saltwater scene.

The best baitcasting models come with a lightweight spool, making it easy to start the spool revolving as line is cast; this also makes the spool easy to stop at the end of the cast. Lightweight materials such as aluminum and magnesium are used in quality reels. Inexpensive reels may have many plastic parts that are prone to failure. Metal parts in any reel are more reliable for keeping the interior gears lined up and synchronized for maximum performance.

Unlike the spinning reel, the baitcasting reel is fixed to the top side of the rod and is very close to the rod blank. This placement gives anglers the ability to put more pressure on a fish. The lower gear ratios common to the baitcasters also equate to more cranking power, which is one of the reasons anglers prefer this type of reel when fishing around structure. One good tip for learning to use a baitcasting reel begins when filling the spool. Instead of filling the spool to within one-eighth inch of the top, leave it down a little further. This will give you a little more forgiveness when learning to cast a revolving spool reel. Once you've mastered the skill of casting you can return to filling the spool to within one-eighth inch of the top to achieve longer casts.

Regardless of the type of reel you choose, either baitcasting or spinning, you should follow Capt. Rick Burns's advice, "Don't buy cheap, it will cost you fish, period!" He believes in using high-quality reels that will do the job and last awhile. He suggests visiting a reel-repair shop to see what advice they can give you. Reel-repair experts know the reels that are most and least reliable, and which are easiest to work on and whether or not repair parts are available. These are all-important considerations in your choice of a new reel.

Reel Maintenance

Reel manufacturers offer advice on their Web sites for reel maintenance and most of it is easily accomplished by the angler without having to take the reel to a shop. Your reel-maintenance kit should include a slot screwdriver, a Phillips-head screwdriver, a soft clean

Reel maintenance can be accomplished with a few simple tools and supplies, and it will improve the performance and longevity of your reel.

towel, cotton swabs, toothbrush, isopropyl rubbing alcohol, and a reel lubricant.

On a spinning reel you can remove the spool from the reel housing by turning the drag knob counterclockwise just as if you were taking the lid off of a jar. This exposes a shaft and gear that you can clean with swabs and alcohol. Also, thoroughly clean the housing of all oil, grease, or salt deposits, and clean the spool itself before replacing. Clean the line roller assembly, and add oil making sure it rolls freely. Remove the crank handle and oil the drive-gear ball bearing that is exposed when the crank is removed. Replace the handle and spool. Reset the drag and you're ready to go.

On a baitcasting reel, remove the spool according to your manufacturer's directions. Use an old toothbrush and alcohol to clean the exterior housing of the reel of any visible dirt or salt deposits. Clean the spool thoroughly and apply oil lightly to the bearing or bushing, whichever is present. The Shimano Web site urges you not to grease the bearings or shaft because it will lessen the free-spooling ability of the reel. Inspect the reel, and oil any shafts, bushings, or bearings that you see. Finally, clean and oil the level-wind system, if it has one, and reassemble the reel.

Repeat these processes anytime you notice that the performance of the reel has changed. The number of times you have to do this will depend on how often you use your reel or how long it remains unused. If for some reason your reel is going to be unused for an extended period of time, it is a good idea to clean and oil it, and then place it in a soft cloth bag for storage. This will keep dust, dirt, and rust from impairing its future use.

For normal maintenance after each fishing trip, a light spray of fresh water will remove salt deposits and dust from your reel. Be careful not to allow the full force of a garden hose to force water inside the reel. This could result in rust and interior damage.

After the light rinsing with fresh water, wipe the reel down with a soft cloth and spray the reel with a water dispersant product such as Reel Magic. This product will lubricate and improve the performance of your reel. Sprayed on your line it will retard line memory, add casting distance, and improve life expectancy of your fishing line.

Inshore specialist Capt. Dale Fields uses a stringent routine to keep his equipment in top shape. "My rods and reels get a minimum of freshwater rinse after every trip. If there was any salt spray they get soap with a soft brush and freshwater rinse. Several times a year, especially during the spring and summer, the reels are washed, dried, and wiped with a protectant such as Rem Oil or a good silicon spray." Rem Oil is a silicone-based gun oil that works great on reels. It acts as a cleaner to remove dirt and grime while displacing non-visible moisture from pores in the metal parts.

If Captain Dale notices a reel is casting poorly, he removes the line and uses 4/0 steel wool on the spool lip to smooth out any rough or irregular spots. He also reminds us that swapping spinning-reel handles to accommodate right- or left-handed users exposes the ball bearings, so they need some light oil occasionally. Once a year he sends his reels to a shop for a complete service.

As an added tip for anglers he says, "I have found that while trailering from one location to another it is best to store rods and reels inside your tow vehicle. All the sand and other debris that comes from the road and gets your boat dirty, also gets on and in your reels."

Endorsing and using these preventive-maintenance suggestions can increase the life of both your rods and reels while avoiding costly repairs and downtime. Use the old adage that an ounce of prevention is worth a pound of cure when scheduling maintenance on your reels. The last thing you want when you get hooked up with the big fish is to have your reel fail.

Last Cast

Choosing the right rod and reel will be one of the most important decisions you have to make about equipment. Captain Myers gives this advice on your selection: "Choose the very best you can afford. Most times you get what you pay for. Do not go for a bargain-brand reel if fishing the salt." Captain Myers would rather buy a somewhat cheaper rod and a more expensive reel. He also warns about buying a reel that is much bigger than you actually need. "If you are only going to fish for reds and trout, a 2500 size is plenty. A 4000 is much heavier and cumbersome and not really necessary. Ask other fishermen who fish a lot what works well for them."

Capt. "Bouncer" Smith fishes Florida's southeastern coast for sailfish, tarpon, snook, king mackerel, dolphin, tuna, and anything else that will come to the bait. If he could choose only one rod to fish for this variety of targets, it would be a 7-foot 20-pound spinning outfit. He chooses a fast-taper rod that has plenty of guts in the lower half to handle the big guys and a light-action tip for enjoying smaller fish and improved casting ability. His offshore reel of choice is a Penn 7500 most of the time. However, he says, "When kite fishing on a sea anchor, we need extra line for multiple sailfish hookups, running in 360 different directions. For this application I would step up to a 9500." All of Bouncer's reels are half filled with 20-pound Tuf Line braid and then topped off with 20-pound Envy Green, Ande mono-filament. This combination allows lots of yardage, good visibility, and the shock-absorbing action and bait-control characteristics of monofilament line.

Given the importance of rod-and-reel selection, Captain Bouncer advises anglers to buy their rods and reels from a small independent dealer with a good reputation and an obvious love of fishing. It is in the dealer's best interest to match the tackle to the angler and his goals in fishing, and they have the expertise to do it. The angler also has a motivation to nurture this relationship because the local guys know, and will share, a lot of additional information about the local fishery.

Captain Van Horn agrees with this philosophy. When buying a new rod and reel, he says, "Go to a small tackle shop or outfitter and ask for advice." The smaller shops often have a more experi-enced staff and more time available for customer service than do big stores. They have a good understanding of the need of local anglers, and they value repeat customers.

Captain McCue advises anglers to match the lightest most-reputable tackle with your primary fishing interest. If you are fishing the flats most of the time he agrees with those who say a smaller reel will do. "When I see people come on board with their own gear, it is often all the high-end stuff currently being pushed by manufacturers and sellers. Much of it is overkill—reels are too big, that hold more than 250 yards of line—and they are heavy to use all day."

Captain McCue carefully balances his reel with a rod. The proce-dure involves installing a reel on a rod and placing your index finger just below the end of the spool. Suspended on that one finger, the rod should balance exactly horizontal to the ground. If it tilts toward the reel, the reel is too heavy. If it tilts toward the rod tip, the rod is too heavy for the reel.

Anglers aboard Captain Bouncer's Dusky 33 will find seven different sets of rods on any given day of fishing. Captain Bouncer says, "No rod-and-reel combination will do everything, and fishing for everything from baitfish to swordfish cannot be done with one outfit. All fishing is fun if the tackle matches the targeted species. The enjoyment is better if the tackle is slightly light instead of too heavy."

3

As Strong as the Weakest Link

Line, Leader, and Terminal Tackle

What's the weakest link between you and a trophy fish at the end of your line? It could be anything from the mainline to the leader to the last thing you tie on your line, which is a single bait hook, multiple hook rigs, or an artificial lure. In between the mainline and the hook or lure there could be a swivel, a snap swivel, a sliding sinker, or maybe even a bobber. Even colored beads can be part of the rig. All are important components for particular types of fishing. The common element here is that the entire rig is only as strong as the weakest link.

No one likes to admit it, but most anglers have experienced the disappointment of losing a fish due to the failure in the fishing line, leader, swivel, a knot, or some other part of the terminal tackle. If it happens to you, just consider it a learning process and try not to let it happen again.

The last time I remember losing a fish because of such a failure was on a nearshore trip to Florida's East Coast. It was summertime, and the big jack crevalle were cruising the bait pods. I was fishing with a 20-pound spinning rod and reel rigged with a single length of 50-pound-test monofilament leader attached to 40-pound braid mainline, which had been doubled with a Bimini twist. On the end of the leader was a Daiichi Bleeding Bait 7/0 circle hook. I pinned a six-inch pogie on the hook and presented it to a school of hungry jacks as they came cruising on a path directly toward the boat.

It didn't take long to get hooked up as the lively pogie settled in front of the marauding jacks, which raced each other for the right to eat the doomed bait fish. As the hook set, the drag screamed, and the fight was on. Hooking one of these big bruising jacks lets you know the pressure a big fish can put on your rig and emphasizes the need for good equipment and strong connections.

After about fifteen minutes in a game of tug-of-war, I decided to tighten up the drag and speed up the landing of the hard-fighting jack. I had barely finished the clockwise motion that tightens the drag when the line went limp. The jack was gone. When I retrieved the line to bait up again, the hook was also gone and a squiggly little pigtail at the end of the leader told the true story. The small adjustment on the drag was just enough to find the weakest link in the rig. The final knot that secured the hook to the leader had failed.

There are really two lessons to be learned from this experience. First, you obviously have to pay careful attention to your knots and tie them correctly. Second, it is the combined strength of all the components of your tackle that helps determine whether or not you land a hooked fish. The final outcome will depend on the action of

Big ocean jacks will test your equipment and may find the weakest link in your tackle. Always double-check your connections.

the rod, the setting of the drag, the strength of the line, the strength of the leader, the quality of snaps and swivels, and the knot itself. Then, all of that will be influenced by the way an angler fights the fish by positioning the rod or palming the spool. Bottom line—there is a whole lot of stuff that can go wrong if not carefully attended to.

The Mainline

Most anglers use one of two varieties of line to fill their spool. The standard for years was the monofilament line manufactured by many different firms. More recently, the so-called super braids are becoming the lines of choice for many of Florida's master anglers.

Monofilament Fishing Line

Monofilament fishing line remains the choice of some anglers. Whether out of personal choice or simply habit, monofilament line is used with great success in many different fishing situations. Mono is an inexpensive line that fits any angler's pocket book, and it has proven itself worthy by performing well on a variety of game fish from spotted sea trout to the mighty tarpon.

On a trip to the Florida Keys in search of tarpon, I boarded a guide's boat and immediately noticed the fluorescent green line that was spooled on the captain's reels. Being an unfamiliar sight to me, I ask why he used the brightly colored line. He explained it was so he could see the line stretched out in front of the boat as he chased the silver kings around and through the bridge pilings where the tarpon feed and flee when hooked. The chase is necessary to keep the fish from cutting off on the structure and also to give the angler a chance to put some line back on the reel.

A confident kind of guy, as most guides are, he simply explained, "You will understand completely when we get hooked up." He was right, I did completely understand a couple of hours later as I sat on the cooler he placed in the front of the center consol. Sitting down was a good idea and the safest way to be involved in the chase that was about to unfold. We floated a live pogie under a natural-color float toward the Channel 2 Bridge near Islamorada. The tide was sweeping in from the Atlantic and out into the Gulf of Mexico. Before reaching the bridge, the float disappeared, the hook was set and the tarpon was flying up out of the water in normal tarpon fashion. A bow to the king and the fight was on. The fluorescent mono could be seen easily as it stretched tightly from the tip of the rod and over the bow of the boat before cutting through the water's surface. The high visibility gave the captain the guidance he needed to maneuver around and through the structure of the double bridges. By following the tarpon, the captain prevented the huge fish from cutting us off on the pilings of the bridge.

Another popular color for some anglers is the red mono, which can actually increase your fishing success. The simple reason is that the color red is the first color to disappear as light penetrates water. So when your lure or bait sinks in the water column, the line becomes less and less visible until it finally disappears. Depending on conditions and technical makeup of the line, it becomes completely invisible by the time it sinks three feet. If the line is invisible to the fish, it will be less likely to spook them from your bait, and you are more likely to hook up.

Monofilament line stretches when pulled and anglers wanting the advantage of the stretch, instead of a broken line, are quick to fill their spool with mono. Guides often use mono when stalking big redfish with inexperienced clients. The forgiving nature of mono makes up for some of the inadequacies of the angler. Every 100 feet of monofilament line will stretch twenty feet before breaking. This stretching does weaken the line, and most guides will replace the line after each day of tangling with large fish.

When you spool your baitcasting reel with new mono, simply feed the line through the eyes of the rod and tie the tag end on to the reel spool using a Uni-Knot with only two wraps. Place a pencil or dowel rod through the spool of new line so the line exits the spool over the top as it revolves. Have a friend hold the pencil and apply slight pressure on the side of the spool to help insure a nice tight wrap onto the reel. Begin to crank the handle to move the new line from the spool to the reel while holding the line tightly between your thumb and forefinger to further ensure the line is wound tightly. Loose mono is an angler's worst enemy, so you want to be sure the line is wound on tight and evenly. Most master anglers advise filling the reel spool until the line is about one-eighth inch from the top of the spool.

To wind new mono on a spinning reel, simply lay the new line on the floor with the label up. Run the tag end through the line guides of the rod and tie the line to the spool with a two wrap Uni-Knot. Make a few turns of the handle to wind the line onto the spool. Keep pressure on the line at all times by running it through your thumb and finger. Stop and lower the rod toward the floor and observe the line between the new spool and the rod tip. If the line continues to form neat circular coils, continue to spool your reel. If the line kinks and winds up on itself, stop and turn over the new spool on the floor and continue the process. The idea is to take the line off the new spool and place it on the reel spool in the same direction it was wound so it does not kink. Continue to place line on the reel until it is filled to about one-eighth inch of the top of the spool.

If you are fishing open waters, such as the flats, your choice of line should be different from fishing around heavy cover. Open-water fishing can be accomplished successfully with 8- to 12-pound mono. If you are fishing structure, you need to beef it up, depending on the size of the fish you expect to catch. You may even want to go to one of the superbraids for their abrasive-resistant quality.

Superbraid Line

The superbraids have been called the lines of the future. Actually, they are the lines of the present for many master anglers and a growing number of everyday recreational anglers. They are smaller in diameter, stronger, and more abrasive-resistant than monofilament lines.

Unlike mono, the superbraids have no stretch to them, and they give the angler a superior feel for the action of the bait and the intensity of the bite. With superbraid line, even subtle bites by wary fish can be detected. This early detection of a bite can prepare the angler to set the hook and seal the deal. Braids also resist the twist that occurs in mono when the angler winds against the drag, which is something the pros don't do but inexperienced anglers do all the time.

A highly desirable characteristic of braided lines is thinner diameter. Twenty-pound Power Pro has the same diameter as 6-pound mono. The thinner diameter allows an angler to place more line on the spool, and for some applications, use a smaller reel than mono would require. The small-diameter braid also comes off the spool easily and flows through the line guides with little friction, which allows longer casts than mono when using light lures and natural baits.

The other advantage of braided lines is the abrasion-resistant character. I have heard more than one angler credit a trophy catch to a superbraid line. These high-tech lines can withstand the wrapping and wearing that can occur around pilings, bridge abutments, and other structure that would cut mono in a heart beat.

For general all-around fishing, Capt. Ed "Jazz" Jazwierski likes to use a Fin-Nor Mega Lite 3000 reel spooled with 20-pound Power

Pro braid. He adds a 30-pound fluorocarbon leader and then the terminal tackle. He says, "I use the 20-pound braid because the reel is used for a variety of situations and not just on the flats. I use it around bridges, in passes, and around docks." Admitting that he looses a little casting distance with the heavier line, he says he just wants to opt for something more than the 8- to 10-pound line that is adequate on the flats. "I also lose some line capacity, but make up for it in abrasion resistance. You never know what may be lurking under your bait and I just like to know that I can apply more pressure and turn 'em away from obstructions."

One drawback to the braids are wind knots. This is a condition that occurs when slack is present in the line and it gets blown into knots and tangles. The same thing happens if you get hung up on the rocks or other structure and have to break loose. If you are pulling hard to sever the connection and the line snaps back at you when it breaks, the ensuing slack line will do all kinds of things you wish it wouldn't. Basically, the line becomes a tangled mess of knots and loops. Sometimes, you can work out the wind knots and get back to fishing, but other times you just have to cut out the knots and start over.

Braided line, like monofilament, can also create a bird nest, which is normally caused by winding some slack line into the reel so it catches the overlaying line on the cast and pulls out the whole mess at once instead of paying out evenly. To avoid a bird nest, you must keep your line tight at all times. The easiest solution is to train yourself to close the bail by hand and lift your rod to pull the line tight before reeling.

Another drawback often cited is the cost of braid. Superbraids cost much more than the same amount of an average monofilament line. However, in the long run they may be cost effective. You certainly don't have to change line after every battle with a large fish, and you can even "turn it around" on your reel spool to get maximum use out of it.

Turning the line around is easier if you have a spare spool for your reel, and if you do have one, replace the spool on your reel with the empty one. Add about twenty to twenty-five feet of monofilament filler to the new spool. Place the spool containing the old line on the floor, run the tag end of the mono through the guides, tie the braided line and mono together, and start winding. Essentially, you end up with brand new line.

By the way, when you spool your reels with new braid, you always want to start with fifteen or twenty yards of mono as a backing or filler. If you don't include the backing, the coils of superbraid will actually spin on the spool, giving you the sensation of a drag that is too loose when a large fish puts pressure on the line. The slippage will not allow you to retrieve the line under pressure.

When reversing an old line, you should put on a little more backing than originally placed on the spool to make up for the braided line that got cut off in rigging and rerigging and cutting out knots. The result should be a spool filled to within one-eighth inch of the edge of the spool.

Capt. Robert McCue, however, deviates from the one-eighth rule. He says one of the keys to distance casting is keeping the spool full to the rim. Even one-eighth of an inch below the spool rim will cause you to loose some distance in casting. Anglers should experiment with this and use what works best for them.

Just as with mono, you want the line to be wound tight and evenly. A big fish will bury the mainline in a loosely spooled reel and actually stop it from feeding out. The result can be a broken line and a lost fish.

The cost of the line is another reason to buy the correct size reel for the fish you target. When you fill a reel that outguns the fish you are targeting, you are wasting expensive braid that will never see the water. Captain McCue says, "When I change the line on a small reel using expensive braid I replace less line than with the bigger ones."

Master anglers agree that the added performance of the superbraid mainlines outweigh the additional cost. If an angler can land that trophy fish after it wrapped around a dock piling, or if a big silver king is hooked in that hard boney mouth because the line didn't stretch on the hookset, the added expense was worth it.

Although braided lines are becoming more and more popular,

anglers have found areas where mono outperforms the braid. For example, Captain McCue uses mono for live-bait fishing for king-fish. "Kings often short-strike and are hooked shallow or in the body with a treble hook. Mono stretches and is more forgiving than braid, which reduces the likelihood of pulling the hook out." Bottom fishing for reef fish such as grouper is another area where anglers prefer mono. Braid is too difficult to break when a fish is under a rock or the bait becomes fouled in a rock.

McCue also cites deep live-bait or jig drifting for tarpon in Boca Grande Pass as an exception to using braid because the thin diameter of the braided line and the strong currents in the Pass combine to create vibrations and actual humming that the fish seem to shy away from. You also have the issue of snagging bottom and breaking. The braid is just too hard to break. Otherwise, says Captain McCue, "Braid is strong, does not stretch, gives more positive hooksets, experiences less line breakage, casts farther, lasts longer, does not spin or get springy after a long fight with a big fish, does not twist after reeling against the drag like mono does on a spinning reel, and you have to change line less often." Actually, that last sentence is quite a testimonial for braided line, but as far as your knowledge base is concerned you need to know the exceptions.

Leaders

Florida's master inshore anglers have three basic materials they use for leader materials. Monofilament is probably the most used, fluorocarbon is becoming more popular, and wire is used for some of the really toothy critters.

The leader is added in saltwater environs to provide a stronger connection close to the fish. Many saltwater species have teeth or at least rough mouths that can nick and chafe a line. This damage can cause the line to break under pressure and the angler to lose a fish. A snook, for example, is a fish that you can lip just as you would a bass—there are no sharp teeth to cause severe harm. You will, however, feel the rough inside of the mouth that can easily chafe and wear on leader material and cause it to weaken and break. Just as a precaution, when handling snook don't forget those razor-sharp gill plates that can cut your line and your flesh. Handle them carefully.

Monofilament line is probably the most popular material for leaders. It is the same line used on reels, only at higher strength when used as a leader. A common example would be a piece of 20-pound mono tied to an 8- to 12-pound mainline of either mono or superbraid. This leader would normally be from 16 to 20 inches long. The longer you make it in the beginning, the more times you can cut and replace the hook or lure without having to replace the entire leader.

Mono is relatively inexpensive and easy to tie to the mainline. Since mono stretches, it protects itself from breakage if a large hard-striking fish comes along.

Fluorocarbon leader material is very similar to mono, but it is more abrasion resistant and is less visible in the water. It's the leader material of choice when you are chasing picky fish, such as snook, that can become leader shy. Fluorocarbon's ability to resist abrasion comes in handy when you need to decrease the pound test in order to get leader-shy fish to bite.

A drawback of fluorocarbon is the price. It costs several times more than monofilament line of equal strength and amount. However, for the added advantage of low visibility and greater strength, most anglers don't mind the added expense.

Master snook anglers will tell you to check your mono or fluorocarbon leader often to be sure it has not been damaged by a previous bite or catch. You can tell quickly if the leader is damaged by running it between your fingers; you want it to feel as smooth as when you tied it on. If it feels rough or nicked, you should cut off that section and rerig. Any knick or abrasion can cause the leader to weaken and fail under the stress of a heavy fish. This warning should apply to any saltwater fish, as most have the ability to damage the leader if the hook is deep and the leader is rubbing on the fish's mouth. Even fins, tails, and gill plates can damage the leader if it comes in contact with them.

Many anglers are guilty of making just one more cast before changing a damaged leader. But if you hook a trophy fish, you

Table 2. Line and Leader Selection

Fish	Line	Leader
Redfish 0–20 lbs	8- to 12-lb test	15- to 20-lb test
Redfish 20-plus lbs	12- to 20-lb test	30- to 40-lb test
Sea Trout	8- to 10-lb test	15- to 20-lb test
Snook 0–10 lbs	8- to 12-lb test	15- to 20-lb test
Snook 10–20 lbs	12- to 20-lb test	30- to 40-lb test
Snook 20-plus lbs	20- to 40-lb test	40-plus-lb test
Tarpon 0–10 lbs	8- to 12-lb test	15- to 20-lb test
Tarpon 10–20 lbs	12- to 20-lb test	30- to 40-lb test
Tarpon 20–40 lbs	20- to 30-lb test	50- to 60-lb test
Tarpon 40–100 lbs	30- to 40-lb test	60- to 80-lb test
Tarpon 100-plus lbs	40- to 50-lb test	80-plus-lb test

Note: Most master anglers would say to use the smallest leader you can get away with. The choices shown here are for open-water fishing. Anglers must adjust accordingly for other conditions. Examples include snook around mangroves or tarpon around bridges. Often, master anglers would upsize both line and leader material from those shown, depending on conditions.

will be sorely disappointed when the leader fails. You should have retied it.

The final leader material we will consider is wire. It can be either single- or multi-strand. Some multi-strand leaders are coated with plastic or nylon. But whether single-strand, coated, or plain cable wire, it is the leader of choice when fishing for really toothy fish such as Spanish mackerel, king mackerel, barracuda, or sharks. These and other saltwater game fish have teeth that will quickly sever ordinary mono or fluorocarbon leaders. If you want to fish for these toothy critters, you will need to take the time to practice the various techniques of making wire leaders.

Using wire also requires a set of tools to cut, pull, and crimp connections. A single multi-tool will do the trick in most cases. For our purposes, we will consider only tied or wrapped rigs. There are many sources that can help you learn the art of wire rigs. Vic Dunaway's *Complete Book of Baits Rigs & Tackle* is an encyclopedia of information on the subject. It includes complete instructions along with outstanding illustrations.

Wire leaders are needed when fishing for toothy fish such as Spanish mackerel, king mackerel (pictured), barracuda, or sharks.

Single-strand wire is preferred by many anglers because of the ease of making connections. The haywire twist will do the job for many inshore applications and can be accomplished without tools. A haywire twist forms a simple loop for attaching a hook or lure and is finished with a tight wrapping of the wire around itself before breaking it off. The process of breaking instead of cutting results in a smoother and safer finish; if the finished end is cut, it leaves a small protruding spike that could result in injury to the angler.

The simplest wire leader is made by using a ball-bearing swivel on one end and a snap swivel on the other. Both swivels can be attached with a haywire twist. The ball-bearing swivel is connected to a normal mono or fluorocarbon leader, and the snap swivel is used to attach hooks or lures. To save time on the water, tie these rigs up before you head out.

Wire cable can be used to accomplish the same connections, but the technique for using twisted-wire cable is more like tying other lines. Normally, the entire setup will include a doubled mainline, a length of heavy monofilament leader, and then the wire rig.

The first cable rig I tied was taught to me by Capt. Keith Kalb-fleisch when we were fishing nearshore Cape Canaveral. He is a true expert when it comes to nearshore fishing with live baits. I had invited Captain Keith along with Capt. Chris Myers aboard my Path-finder so they could teach some tricks of the trade for fishing the beach.

A nearshore fishing excursion usually starts off by cast-netting some bait and then running out to cruise the beach and look for fish. Captain Keith likes to use single hook "stingers" as opposed to treble hook rigs on his nearshore slow-trolling excursions. The single hooks, he says, are safer and just as productive. He also prefers rigging with plain-wire cable as opposed to one that is coated. He feels the knots on plain wire are more dependable. By making the rigs yourself, you can fit them to the size of the bait to be used. For most applications Captain Keith ties a 6/0 Daiichi Octopus hook on the back and a 4/0 on the front of the rig before attaching the wire to a 50-pound monofilament leader. The hooks are attached using a wire snell knot. Captain Keith has an excellent illustration of the knot on his Web site at www.capt-keith.com. The distance between the hooks is determined by the size of the bait. If large tarpon have been spotted rolling you might want to increase your mono leader to 80-pound test.

If your bait is a pogie, for example, the front hook should penetrate the hard part of the nose above the mouth and in front of the eyes. The trailing hook should be pinned through the pogie's back. It is important to have the wire long enough between the hooks to allow a little slack, which allows the baitfish to continue to swim naturally.

In reality, it is probably better to make the rigs up in advance and have them ready to tie directly to your mainline. That includes tying the mono leader to the wire ahead of time also. If you have a spare handy when you get broken off or need to replace a damaged rig, all you have to do is tie the mono leader to your doubled mainline. Don't forget to make up the wire part of the rigs in different lengths to accommodate different-size baits. I mark mine small, medium, and large with most of the pre-made rigs in the medium size, which will accommodate six- to eight-inch bait fish, the prevalent size used in my area.

Fishing Knots

As mentioned before, there are plenty of things that can go wrong between you and a big fish. Of all those things, poorly tied knots are probably the number one reason for lost fish. Don't ever take knots for granted. Do everything in your power to ensure a carefully tied knot at every connection. Even a well-tied knot will become weaker after being tested by a bruising saltwater fish. This means it's a good idea to retie your connections after fighting and boating any oversized fish. And, you certainly should retie all your knots before starting your next day's fishing adventure.

Given the amount of preparation that a successful fishing trip requires, it's not asking too much to expect anglers to learn a few basic knots. You don't have to know every knot in the universe, but

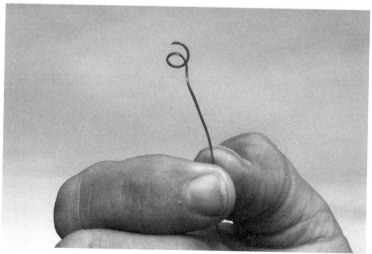

When you lose a big fish and are left with a pigtail on the end of your line, you know your knot has failed.

knowing just a few appropriate for your own fishing interests will make you a more successful angler. Once you learn the knots, the question every angler should ask is, "Which knot do I use and when do I use it?"

Knots come with all kinds of names, some rather exotic and others simply descriptive of the knot-tying process. Common knots include the Bimini twist, the Uni-Knot, spider hitch, end loop knot, surgeon's knot, and the improved clinch knot, to name only a few. The Internet will provide all the information you need to become a seasoned knot tier. There are plenty of books and CDs on the market as well that can help you learn the knots you need.

When considering knots, an angler should once again consider the size of the fish he is targeting. Most master anglers prefer to use small diameter braided line as the mainline and add a shock leader to provide added strength and abrasion resistance and the ability to withstand the physical impact of a hard strike.

The small diameter of today's high-tech braided line sometimes makes it necessary to provide a doubled line before attaching the leader. One of the most common, although relatively harder to tie, doubling procedures is the Bimini twist. Others include the spider hitch, a Uni-Knot, and finally, a simple fold of the mainline before tying a knot.

A survey of twenty master anglers revealed that the knot used most often to double mainline is the Bimini twist. A double line is normally used when the possibility of catching predators of 20 pounds or more is likely, which necessitates the need for a shock leader of adequate size. The double line adds overall strength to the rig and provides the basis of a stronger knot at the leader. When the leader is several times stronger than the mainline, the doubled mainline reduces the difference between the two and results in a stronger knot. Small lines connected to larger lines can actually cut through and weaken the knot.

Capt. Jim Savaglio, who grew up on Long Island, doubles his mainline when fishing for tarpon or snook. On the low end, he uses 12-pound mono but will increase to 30-pound mono as the fishing warrants. "The knot I use is a Bimini twist. I find the Bimini knot provides a shock-absorbing section as well as added strength to the line." When he uses the Bimini twist, he still uses an appropriate length of leader, preferring fluorocarbon, before attaching the terminal tackle.

Two other popular knots used to produce the double mainline are the Uni-Knot and the spider hitch. The Uni-Knot application for doubling uses a separate piece of the mainline for the doubled part and is connected to the mainline using a regular Uni-Knot.

The spider hitch is a faster and easier way to create a double line. It is not, however, recommended for lines greater than 30-pound test. The spider hitch is said to be as strong as the Bimini, but does not withstand a sharp snapping bite so well. As noted before, any knot is more likely to fail if snapped suddenly, as opposed to straight pulling pressure.

Captain Jazz prefers the spider hitch for doubling a monofilament mainline. "I like to use a spider hitch for doubling mainline, because it is quick and easy, even in the dark, unlike a Bimini twist." Captain Jazz says the double line and added leader act like a shock absorber for the mainline. His fishing activities lead him to use up to 60-pound mono for the leader. "I have had fish wrap around a dock piling, mangrove, or some other structure and break one side of the double line, and we still brought the fish to the boat on one strand."

Here is how Captain Jazz adds the leader. Double about fifteen to twenty-four inches of the mainline and tie a spider hitch. Put the rod in a rod holder. From just under the spider hitch, slide your fingers down the double line until you have a small loop at the end, and tie on the leader with an Albright knot. "I like to have tension on the mainline when I tie the leader so it will be straight and both strands are used equally as a shock absorber." Using the Albright knot should ensure a continued hookup even if one side of the double line breaks. The greater the poundage of the leader, the fewer wraps you will need to make the knot clinch down tight. Practice with different-size mono to find the number of wraps that result in a smooth, tight finished knot.

Capt. Ray Markham fishes the Tampa area and often with very

light line. He uses a simple form of doubling the mainline. He folds over about twelve to fourteen inches of the mainline so that it is doubled and then ties a double Uni-Knot to attach the leader. Trim off the excess line, and you have double line directly at the knot but not above it. Especially with braid, this method reduces the chances that the mainline will cut through the leader. When using mono Captain Markham often ties these knots on 2- to 4-pound-test line. When he uses braid, he adds a 20-pound mono or fluorocarbon leader by folding 8-pound Power Pro and tying the double Uni-Knot. He doubles the mainline for one reason: greater knot strength.

Capt. Rick Grassett is also a proponent of the fold. He says to double the mainline by simply folding about a one-foot section over and work with a doubled piece of line to tie the leader to the mainline (no knot above the doubled section). "I double the mainline to minimize the chances of the braid cutting through my leader. For snook and redfish tie 10- to 20-pound braid to a 30-pound fluorocarbon leader. If tarpon are the target, start with 50-pound braid and add an 80-pound fluorocarbon leader."

Any of these knots can be used successfully, but as mentioned before, the number-one choice of master anglers is the Bimini twist. A little practice with tying this knot will make it much easier to rig, and its performance is worth the trouble. Rather than trying to tie it by looking at pictures of the Bimini, find a fellow angler who can show you how to tie it. This hands-on instruction, passed on from one angler to another, will shorten the learning curve considerably.

Regardless of whether the mainline is doubled or not, the next important connection is line-to-leader. Any of the following knots can be used to attach the mainline to the leader. Generally the knots described can be use with braid up to 40-pound test and mono up to 80. Once an angler moves to stronger grades of mono, it is probably wise to learn to crimp your connections.

One knot stands out here as an overall favorite for tying line to leader. The Uni-Knot can quickly and efficiently provide the strong connection needed between the mainline and the leader. It can be used with both single or double mainline with no need to learn separate knots for each. I use this knot exclusively for line-to-leader connections, except when the size of the leader is considerably larger than the mainline.

Suppose you wanted to add a 50-pound mono leader to a 12-pound mainline. The knot to use here is the Albright special. This knot provides a strong reliable connection, while still producing a small profile. In fact, the profile of this knot is so small you can wind a long mono leader through the guides on most rods and on to the reel. A long leader can be a great advantage on large fish, especially close to the boat. It can even allow you to tighten the drag and give you a larger-diameter line to grab hold of when landing the fish.

Typically, however, this heavy leader will be only about four or six feet long depending on your application. This length will work well on tarpon, king mackerel, and large jacks on the beach. If you are using wire stinger rigs, as needed for the kingfish and other toothy critters, the same Albright knot used to tie leaders can be used to tie on the wire.

Next, a connection needs to be made between the leader and the hook or lure. There are several popular knots used for this purpose. Most of them provide a connecting knot pulled up tight to the terminal tackle, except for one that is called a loop knot.

The simple improved clinch knot is a reliable knot that is used often for terminal tackle. It is created by inserting the tag end of the leader through the hook or lure, making a few twists, running the tag end through two loops, and pulling up tight. Don't forget to lubricate all knots by pulling them through your mouth before cinching to the terminal tackle. This knot is so simple even kids can learn to tie it quickly, and the end product is a very reliable knot. Other knots such as the Uni-Knot or the Palomar knot will accomplish the same thing.

If you want to supply a looser knot that allows the lure or bait a little more play at the point of contact, a loop knot will do the trick. There are many versions, and you should experiment with them and find one you can tie easily and efficiently. You can't catch a fish while tying knots, so you want to be able to construct them as quickly as possible. The advantage of the loop knot is that it does not slip

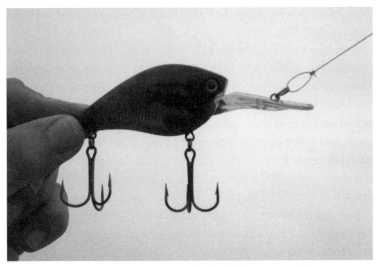

A loop knot will allow your lure or bait hook a little more wiggle room.

down to the hook or lure, leaving the hook or lure freedom to slide around the loop. The idea is to provide live bait more wiggle room and artificial baits more action. Once I learned a loop knot, I used it for almost every application of a direct connection to a hook or lure.

Other Hardware

Swivels and Split Rings

Swivels and snap swivels are often used as a connecting device between the mainline and leader. They connect lines easily with simple knots and eliminate twist between the mainline and the hook or lure. And a twisting line is something you want to avoid; spiraling or spinning baits can twist the mainline, reducing its performance.

When you retrieve a shrimp, it will spin and cause twist in a monofilament line. The addition of a swivel will reduce the transfer of the spiraling bait to the main fishing line. Some master anglers will pinch off the tail of the shrimp before pinning it on the hook.

This not only reduces the spin on the retrieve, but makes it more aerodynamic in casting.

Metal spoons also are major contributors to line twist. When retrieved too fast, spoons will spin instead of wobble. Without a swivel, all that spinning is transferred to the leader and then to the mainline, and this causes poor performance and weaker line. Master anglers get around this problem by adding a swivel directly to the spoon using a split ring to make the attachment. Special pliers are available to easily open and attach the split ring, first to the swivel and then to the spoon. If you use spoons, it is a good idea to attach the swivels before even getting on the water to save time when choosing a spoon for your next bait. These same split rings can be used to replace worn hooks on lures or to change the size of the hooks on your favorite lures.

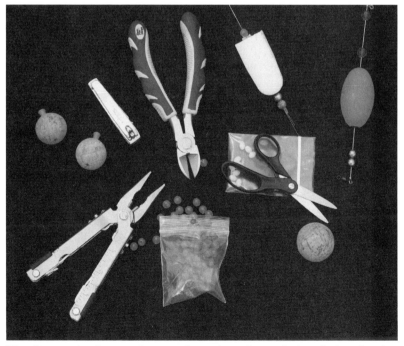

Miscellaneous hardware and accessories such as pliers, swivels, split rings, beads, and floats are sometimes needed in special fishing applications.

Floats

Floats or bobbers are another part of an angler's inshore tackle box. Popping corks have been used for years to float live shrimp over shallow grass flats in search of gator sea trout. In more recent years, the popping cork has been redesigned to include brass or plastic beads that produce a clacking sound to attract fish to the bait. Today, the bait dangling below the bobbers is often artificial instead of live, and such rigs are used with great success.

The D.O.A. Clacker is a float that uses plastic beads to cause a rattling sound that attracts fish. The beads are strung on a heavy wire run vertically though the float. The wire may include a lead weight on the bottom side of the float to make it cast farther and float upright for easy visibility.

D.O.A. sells a pre-rigged clacker with one of its signature shrimp already attached to a mono leader. It is called the Deadly Combo. Whether you make it yourself or use the pre-rigged version, be sure to make good connections. If you are using mono, a simple clinch knot will work fine from the mainline to the float, float to leader, and leader to bait. Of course the bait could be any live or cut bait for which you need a hook, or it could be any one of numerous plastic baits, including the plastic shrimp that is included in the pre-rigged combo.

If you use braid for your mainline, you should consider attaching a short piece of 15- to 20-pound mono leader between the mainline and the float with a Uni-Knot for the mainline to the leader and a clinch knot from the leader to the float. This will make a very secure connection to the topside of the float. If you don't want to add the mono, use a Uni-Knot instead of the clinch knot to make the connection from the braided mainline to the float. The remainder of the rig is the same as described above.

Natural-cork floats are used by many tarpon guides in the keys. The purpose of the float is to keep a live baitfish high in the water column as it is swept with the current toward a likely tarpon haunt. The natural color of the float does not present any undue distraction to wary predators.

The simplest of all the floats is the plain old red-and-white bob-ber with a push-button attachment. If you want to suspend bait at a certain level in the water, you can add this old standby in a jiffy. It is also useful if you need to add a little weight to gain extra cast-ing distance. In fact, some versions of this float are designed to fill with water to add even more weight. They are usually constructed of transparent material that adds the element of invisibility to the rig. The other advantage of these push-button floats is that they do not require another connection and do little to weaken the rig.

Beads

Colored plastic beads are often used in special-application fishing rigs. They can act like a shock absorber to maintain connections when friction could cause damage to a knot or line. The beads also add color, which can be instrumental in attracting fish.

A popular use of a bead as a shock absorber is in the slip-sinker rig used to allow a fish to pick up bait and run without pulling the sinker's weight, which could compel the fish to let go. There are dif-ferent variations of the rig so I will describe a common one. The materials needed are a swivel, a plastic bead, a piece of leader mate-rial, a barrel sinker, and a hook.

Starting with the mainline in hand, run it through the barrel sinker and then through the bead. Attach the swivel to the mainline using a clinch knot. (If you are using braid as the mainline, you might want to add a three-foot or longer section of mono before stringing the sinker and the bead.) Next, tie a fourteen- to sixteen-inch mono leader to the swivel, and attach your hook to the end of the leader. Once the rig is baited and cast, a fish can pick up the bait and swim away without feeling the weight of the sinker. The bead will protect the knot on the top side of the swivel from damage as the sinker slides up and down the mainline and bangs against the bead instead of the knot.

Capt. Tom Van Horn uses the slip-sinker rig when fishing for giant black drum in the Indian River Lagoon. Baits of choice are extra-large shrimp, blue crabs (either whole or cut in half), or fresh

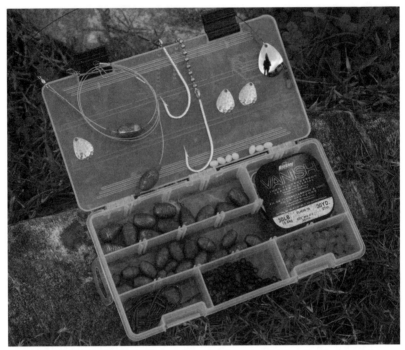

A simple plastic tackle box will store barrel sinkers, hooks, beads, chains, and other accessories.

clams, with the shells thrown out as chum. Since these drum are "shell crackers," scraping a few barnacles off the bridge pilings can sweeten up the bite. Use heavy tackle and be prepared to use the boat's engine to help pull these big bruisers away from the bridge pilling once hooked up.

This chapter has touched on only a few of the many rigs used in fishing, but these are some of the most-often-used rigs for chasing common species in Florida such as snook, redfish, tarpon, and sea trout.

In my opinion the most important part of the whole chapter is the knot section. The way you become proficient with knots is to practice tying them, and once you are proficient, you can create any of the rigs discussed above and many more.

Last Cast

When it comes to knots, Captain McCue says a fisherman needs to know only one knot. He says that one knot is the Uni-Knot. "I double all of my fishing line before connecting it to the shock leader. The purpose of doubling is to increase the material used in tying two different diameters together. By increasing the material of the main fishing line, I feel the knot 'bites' better and results in a more positive connection."

He says you need only a few inches of the doubled mainline to perform the task. "In my charter fishing, I use fourteen-pound Fire-line or Stealth Spiderwire for general flats fishing—snook, redfish, trout, and such. I prefer Power Pro fifty- or sixty-five-pound test for tarpon fishing. I use sixty-pound mono for grouper bottom fishing, fifty-pound mono for fishing deep in Boca Grande Pass for tarpon,

Large Indian River black drum are often caught on slip-sinker rigs. Use a circle hook baited with blue crap or jumbo shrimp.

and twenty-five-pound mono for slow trolling live baits for king-fish."

Captain McCue's success with only one knot proves that rigging can be simple, but never forget your terminal tackle is only as strong as its weakest link.

4

How Do You Get to Carnegie Hall?

The Art of Practice

There is an axiom that practice makes perfect. Practice tying knots and you will get very good at tying them; practice casting and you will get very good at casting. If you are willing to practice when you are not fishing, it's likely to produce huge dividends when you do fish. There is also plenty of time to practice when you are fishing, if you are willing to do it. In this chapter our master anglers reveal some great tips for practicing your fishing skills both on and off the water.

Whether fishing with a buddy, spouse, or tournament partner, anglers are often part of a team, and the success of the team depends on the skills of the individual members. No specialists here. Capt. Bouncer Smith says a good team is made up of individuals who can play different positions. Being able to play all the positions well requires practice.

Memory experts tell us that it is intensive repetition that perfects our skills such as knot tying, casting, or for that matter, riding a bicycle. You need to approach the task seriously, and practice it over and over again if you want to embed it in your mind and generate a capacity to complete a given task without having to think about it.

Once you have tied a Uni-Knot a hundred times or so, you don't have to think about it anymore. You just do it. Once you have made a 50-foot cast in your backyard time and time again, you can make that same cast on the water when it really counts. Practice is all about repetition of the task and the willingness to engage in it.

When we asked some of the Florida guides to name skills that would help weekend anglers improve as fishermen, knot tying was high on the list. Captain Bouncer said, "For anglers to become better fishermen they must learn to tie good knots and wrap wire. This takes a lot of land-based practice." He says the way you practice is to "Tie, tie, tie, and tie." It's not enough to tie up ten wire stinger rigs and put them in your tackle box for when you need them next. You really need to take a special interest in developing the new skill and stick with it. Tie up ten rigs, cut them apart, and tie them again. Serious repetition will soon make you an expert.

With any kind of knot practice, take the trouble to figure out how each knot works and why one doesn't look like the previous one. For example, when I started using the Albright knot to connect wire to heavy mono I noticed that each knot did not look the same. I examined my procedure and found that if I didn't hold all the coils of mono well back behind the loop in the wire, some would fall over the front when drawn tight and produce a different, weaker knot. With practice I learned to wind the coils tighter and hold those coils back with my fingers when cinching the knot to its final form.

I want to say it one more time: The main element in learning and developing skills is repetition, which brings us back to the question that is the title of this chapter. "How do you get to Carnegie Hall?" The answer, of course, is, "Practice, practice, practice." And, if you want to get even better, you should practice some more.

Visualization

Visualization can be described as a technique for creating images in your mind that result in the successful accomplishment of a goal. Captain Bouncer recalls that his friend Capt. Marsha Bierman, who's traveled the globe in search of the world's largest game fish, tells her seminar audience to practice in their head. The idea is to visualize what needs to be done to complete any fishing activity at the highest level of skill. He says, "It could be anything—going to the rod, engaging the drag, winding, etc. Any angler can practice dropping back, winding tight, pumping and winding, the list is endless." Captain Bouncer says, "To become a better fisherman, anglers need to practice all of the above, plus learn how to work all their electronics, handle the boat, net a fish, gaff a fish, throw a cast net, etc., etc., etc."

Well, that's a long list of things to practice, so how can visualization help anglers improve their fishing skills? Capt. Jim Savaglio uses the analogy of a golfer getting ready to make a shot and making visualization a part of his pre-swing routine. "I usually characterize my 'practice swing' as the setting up of a spinning reel allowing the correct amount of line or leader to drop, followed by the visualization of where I would like the bait to land, then a few deep breaths and the wind up and release."

Captain Savaglio adds that the visualization should always be positive. "Don't think about throwing in the mangroves, that's negative reinforcement. Think about getting a triple skip of the bait under the mangrove, giving you the double advantage of a stunned baitfish and more distance up under the trees." It is best to have a particular goal in mind. He says, "I practice in my mind, missing the lowest branch of the mangroves or throwing to within inches of the feeding pop of a snook." The beauty of this technique is that you can do it anywhere.

Bradenton's Capt. Merrily Dunn also uses visualization as a means to practice casting. She says, "This is a technique that allows you to practice anywhere, anytime, and you don't have to be embarrassed while doing it." She says to begin with a gripping fist but without a rod. Put your casting forearm out in front of you with your elbow straight. Pull your forearm toward your shoulder, pretending you have your rod in hand. Stop. Now push your forearm forward, and stop just before you actually straighten that elbow. Remember to keep your wrist straight, no bending, or your practice will not help your stroke once you pick up the rod. You have just made a false stroke without a rod. What you are doing is teaching your mind and muscles to remember the stroke, so once you get a rod in your hand, it will be second nature. Captain Merrily is describing the visualization of a fly-rod technique, but it would work just the same for any type of casting. Visualizing a perfect cast is simply practicing it in your mind.

Casting Practice

Casting is considered by many as the most important aspect of fishing, and you can practice it even when you are not on the water. In fact, casting deserves all the practice time you can afford to give it.

Basic Casting

If you are sight-fishing with a guide, you may hear instructions like, "Forty feet at two o'clock." The guide would be telling you to cast out forty feet in the direction of two o'clock relative to the bow of the boat, which is always at twelve o'clock and not the direction your feet are facing. When the guide says "forty feet," fifty feet is too far, thirty feet is too short, and don't confuse two o'clock with ten o'clock. You need to carry out the instructions as closely as possible to have a decent chance at hooking the fish.

Capt. Dave Sutton refers to this clock system as a direction finder between the guy on the platform and the angler on the boat. "So many times, my nine o'clock is my angler's three o'clock. It would also be very advantageous to have a better understanding of where ten-thirty is—especially when twenty bonefish have just appeared and are coming toward the boat at only thirty feet away."

Captain Sutton suggests practicing the clock system in your head as you are walking down the street. The direction you are walking is twelve o'clock. Pick out a target at eleven o'clock and count down in half-hour segments as you approach your target. Ten-thirty. Ten. Nine-thirty. When your target is directly on your left, bingo, nine o'clock. A quick response to your partner's directions on where to cast will often make the difference in hooking up or not.

If you are fishing on your own, you are not receiving instructions from someone else but are processing the task in your own mind. If you see the fish yourself instead of being instructed by the guide, you know instinctively what to do—you just have to do it. To be sure that you can just do it, you should practice making that thirty- or forty-foot cast before you go fishing. Your backyard or a nearby park are good places to practice. You don't really need anything other than your rod and reel and a hula-hoop. The two main things to consider are the size of the target and the distance of the cast. You should practice until you can hit the target consistently at various distances.

Capt. John Bunch adds another dimension to casting practice that emphasizes the importance of being able to cast low, such as under the mangroves or other structure. He suggests tying a clothesline between two trees to create a casting range. Tie the line low enough to simulate casting under mangroves or other overhanging structure such as docks. After you have completed a few hundred repetitions on your newly created casting range, take the hook off of an old gold spoon and continue your practice on the water by completing some reality casting to the mangroves. He also stresses the importance of standardized line for your day-to-day use. He says, "I throw twenty- to thirty-pound Power Pro. I don't fish the mangroves with anything else." The point is, if you use 20- to 30-pound Power Pro when you fish, use it when you practice too.

Wind is a major factor you must consider in casting. The stronger the wind, the more difficulty you will have in hitting the target. Your practice should include all types of weather conditions, including the wind. Capt. Ed "Jazz" Jazwierski likes to take the outfit he uses most often and practices with it on a windy day. He suggests tying on your favorite lure minus the hooks and make casts toward various objects in an open area. He uses a large churchyard near his home. "I'll make casts to the available landscaping such as orange trees, hedges, and other bushes. I cast towards objects from different angles until I am making consistent casts, then I move back ten to fifteen feet and repeat the process. It's great practice and you learn how the wind can affect your casts. Many anglers do not compensate for the wind before they cast, resulting in a hooked dock or mangrove."

As Captain Jazz suggests, you should always practice with the rod and reel you expect to be using under similar circumstances. Your goal should be to gain complete familiarity with your equipment so that you know what to expect from it.

For purposes of this discussion the popular spinning rod and reel will be the rod of choice. If you are right handed, pick up the rod with your right hand and place the stem of the reel between your second and third fingers. With your left hand, carefully rotate the spool until the line comes to its closest distance to the rod. At this point you should easily be able to pick up the line with your forefinger and press it tightly to the rod. Open the bail with your left hand. The line should be coming straight up from the top side of the spool and held tight under your finger. You are now ready to cast.

Point the rod in the direction you want to cast, with your arm bent at the elbow and forearm at 90 degrees to your body. Raise the rod in one motion to slightly behind vertical, and snap your wrist forward to "load" the rod and add distance to your cast. This is where practice becomes very important. You must learn when to release the line from under your finger. With practice you will find the exact time to release the line to allow the lure or bait to launch

When preparing for a cast, turn the spool until the line is at its closest proximity and parallel to the rod. Pick up the line with your finger, open the bail, and you are ready to cast. As shown in the top photo, the line should go directly from the finger to the spool. The slack shown in the bottom photo is what you want to avoid.

toward your target, whether that target is a hula-hoop or a sighted fish.

Inexperienced casters tend to propel the bait in too large an arc, with the lure ascending very high before descending toward the intended target. If you can imagine this scenario of a high-arching cast, it is quickly apparent that a windy day will play havoc with your cast. Once the bait hits the water, the line is arcing high above and the line will carry with the wind, creating a huge amount of slack line between you and the bait. If you get a quick strike and try to set the hook, you will get nothing but the slack. To avoid this slack, you must eliminate the high-arching cast, especially when casting on windy days. It is like a double-edged sword—the wind makes the target harder to hit and also produces slack-line between you and any potential hookup. Practicing under windy conditions can improve your accuracy and eliminate the excess slack.

Capt. Chris Myers, of Florida Fishing Lessons, uses and teaches a method of casting that is especially useful on the Florida flats. He describes it as more of a sidearm or three-quarter-arm cast. The lower rod position, coming from the side instead of overhead, immediately takes some of the arc out of the line. Captain Myers says, "No matter what bait or lure you choose, if you can't place it in front of the fish, it will never work. Casting accuracy is an important skill that, unfortunately, few take time to master. The time to practice your casting is not when you are facing a school of hungry fish; this is when an accurate cast should be second nature."

According to Captain Myers, "The number one reason people don't catch more fish is their lack of casting skills." He suggests practicing your casting on days when you are not fishing. Poor weather days, for example, are an excellent time to practice. You can set up simple casting drills in your backyard by placing targets at varying distances and angles. He says you should always use two hands when casting forehand to achieve greater distance and accuracy. Since the zone of interest for many fish is relatively small, you should practice casting to small targets. Captain Chris suggests using lures or casting plugs of varying weights and sizes to mimic different fishing conditions. He also suggests casting from various positions such as sidearm, overhand, and backhand, since you may not always be in the same position to cast. Move your feet to the most favorable position to make the cast you want.

Captain Chris controls the mainline with his index finger. Recognizing that all anglers pinch the line against the rod when the bail is open and then release the line to cast, he says it's what you do with your finger after the release that matters most. He controls the line by lightly touching it with his finger around the first knuckle as it exits the reel. The closer you move your finger toward the rod, the more pressure you apply to the line and the slower your lure will travel. He uses this method to stop errant casts short by catching the line in the fold of his knuckle and to make desired casts land exactly where he wants them to. He says, "Stopping the line with your finger also allows an angler to move the lure with the rod, while reaching up with the other hand to close the bail. This method is very effective when casting with a crosswind, since it allows you to maintain constant pressure on the line and prevent the wind from creating a bow in the line."

Captain Myers also suggests conducting practice while fishing. He says, "Never get into a routine of blind-casting. Always pick some sort of target. It may be a pod of baitfish, a wake, a sand patch, or just a spot you focus on with your eyes. Using this method with every cast is practicing your accuracy." He operates by a simple slogan, "The better you cast, the more you will catch."

"Fish only eat with one end of their bodies," says Capt. Blair Wiggins, summing up the importance of casting well. "You can't be behind the fish; you have to be in front of them. The way you do that consistently is the same way you get to Carnegie Hall. You have to practice, practice, practice.

Practice Casting Made Fun

Practice does not have to be a chore. In fact, it should be a labor of love, and it can be made fun by incorporating games. Or, gather a buddy or two and head for the park for some friendly competition. Practice is usually accomplished with hookless casting plugs available from various retailers. You can also make your own by simply taking the hooks off an old plug or bending the hook closed on a rigged plastic bait.

Competition can be as simple as measuring distance—he who casts the greatest distance wins. You can use six- or eight-foot lengths of rope to mark off various distances and cast from a fixed position behind another piece of rope. Just by making it competitive, you begin to think about all the things that are important to distance casting such as arm position, hand placement, wrist snap, line size, reel maintenance, etc. Competing with your friends actually develops skills and techniques that probably would not be developed practicing on your own.

Another way to involve competition is to cast to five or more round targets such as a hula-hoop. Place the hoops at various distances from a fixed line demarcating where each competitor casts. Each person makes two casts at each target from behind the line. A rotation is established from right to left moving anglers through the course. The process is repeated until all anglers have complete two rounds.

A typical scoring procedure will give 6 points when the first cast lands in the target, 4 points when the second cast lands in the target and zero points if both casts miss. In organized competitions, the field is limited to five or six anglers in each round. This competition is referred to as *skish*, and both accuracy and distance are necessary for success.

Casting practice should include visualizing what different distances look like. Take time to actually measure distances to a target, and arrange them so they are easily remembered. For example measure out thirty feet to a hula hoop, then measure the next one at forty feet. Finally, measure out another at fifty. Visualize and think about these distances in relation to each other, and take a picture of the distance in your mind as you practice. On a different day, measure them out at three different distances and repeat the process.

Competition or not, the resulting practice will make you a better angler. Don't take casting for granted; it's just too easy to spend a little time each week in perfecting your skills and technique in this

Regardless of whether you practice casting for competition or pleasure, the train-ing will make you a better angler.

important part of angling. If you practice your casting, your fishing success will improve, whether you are casting artificial lures from a boat or natural bait from the shore.

Cast Netting

For live-baitfishermen, the ability to throw a cast net is an impor-tant skill they can acquire. Cast netting is an art that is more easily demonstrated then described on paper. Valuable fishing time can be wasted by an inexperienced cast netter, so like other elements of the fishing adventure, practice before you get on the water.

A good way to begin learning the rudiments of cast netting is to watch a video, such as the one developed by Calusa Cast Nets. The video can be purchased online at calusa.com. In fact, you can view the first chapter online. The video goes through every step you need to know, including how to select, maintain, and most important,

Cast nets are used for collecting many species of Florida bait fish. Quality nets lie flatter in the water and sink faster than poorly designed nets.

throw a net successfully. Throwing a cast net is like anything else; the more you practice, the easier it gets.

Captain Merrily is a proponent of honing your cast-netting skills. She suggests a few questions you should answer as you practice. First, can you throw a bigger one? Remember, the bigger the net the more coverage you get. With a bigger net, you can throw fewer times and get more bait. Secondly, how heavy a net do you throw? If you throw lighter nets in shallow water and heavier nets in deeper water, you need to practice both. She suggests practicing in areas where it is easy to retrieve the net. The backyard lawn is a good place to practice, but just remember you aren't on the deck of your boat tossing over a trolling motor or railing. Set up obstacles to simulate the real thing. At least, while practicing in the grass, you don't get wet.

A few things to look for in buying a cast net include the rope, the net itself, the amount of weight, and the construction design. The rope should be of a fairly large diameter to easily handle and coil in the throwing process and long enough to catch bait in deeper water. Some master anglers will actually add a length of rope, if necessary, to bring bait up from very deep water. The rope should also be soft and not too stiff. The net should be made from high-quality monofilament mesh to ensure a soft pliable net that will lie flat when thrown.

Most master anglers want a net with at least 1½ pounds of lead per foot of net. This means a 12-foot net will weigh no less than 18 pounds. This weight is needed to make the net sink fast before the bait has a chance to swim out from under it. Finally, you want to select a net that is constructed in triangular segments. When expanded to its open position, a quality net will look like a big pie with each piece of the pie being one element in the overall design. Nets constructed with this triangular design will lay flat, cover more water, and be more effective than other configurations.

Sonar and Navigating Technology

Capt. Robert McCue uses his GPS to establish his own private baitfish fishery. After locating bait through conventional methods, like seeing dimpling water or diving birds, he marks the spot with his GPS. Over time he has accumulated and recorded numerous locations, many unique to him, where he has caught baitfish before and expects to get them in the future. This electronic assistant gives him confidence that he will be able to find the bait quickly on his next outing.

Practicing with your electronics, or better yet, studying all their functions and knowing how to use them, is another wise investment of time away from the water. Anglers certainly don't want to waste valuable fishing time trying to figure out how to use their GPS units to navigate to the current fishing hot spot. Using the GPS needs to be second nature, and practicing before you get on the water is the key.

Most modern fish finder–GPS units come with either built-in simulation, a Web site, or a CD that provides the tools you need to practice its operation. Get familiar with the menu that connects

GPS or sonar electronics can take the guesswork out of finding your fishing locations. You can learn to use them on your home computer.

you to the various functions such as sensitivity, split screen, depth range, etc., that you will want to use when fishing. Also, familiarize yourself with the navigation features that allow you to instantly mark a waypoint when you hook a fish or set a route to a new fishing destination. These are all things you need to practice through repetition, so when the need arises on the water you automatically push the right button and don't waste valuable time.

The Art of Observation

Observation is another characteristic commented on by many of the guides participating in this book. Observation is more than just looking around; it is an art that anglers can practice to improve their fishing skills. It is the act of looking at different recognizable occurrences in a way that adds to their fishing knowledge base. Observations are made by using your five senses. Snook fishermen instinctively know the popping sound of a feeding snook and cast in that direction. Hearing the pop helps them locate the fish. Sight-fishing anglers watch for tails sticking out of the water, or wakes pushed by moving fish to locate their prey. Black-drum anglers can locate fish around bridges by listening for the drumming sound made by the fish.

Given that your eyes will be the most important tool in observing conditions around you, a quality pair of polarized sunglasses is a good investment. Polarized sunglasses reduce reflections off the water and give you a better view of fish and other underwater objects. Good polarized sunglasses will not only improve your ability to see fish underwater, but also protect your eyes from the sun's damaging rays. Capt. Rick Burns advises, "Arm yourself with a good pair of sunglasses and keep your baby blues open for any abnormal signs that may indicate the presence of fish." He also suggests wearing a wide-brim hat to shade your eyes for additional protection from the sun and improved visibility.

The art of observation, in the sense we are using it here, does not come naturally for most folks. You have to think about it. You have to practice it. Even when you are not on the water fishing you can

Good polarized sunglasses are a must for serious anglers—they improve your vision on the water and protect your eyes from the sun's harmful rays.

practice observation skills, which you can use later when you are on the water. Capt. Dale Fields says one of the most important factors in practicing anything is patience. Basically, you need to increase your patience, slow down, watch, and listen for what is going on around you.

You can strengthen your observation skills when driving to work or to some other destination by paying close attention to your physical surroundings and making mental notes along the way. Start off with a question relating to what, when, where, or how some particular event occurred. A sample question might be, "Where are the gas stations on my route today?" Or, "What are the characteristics of the stations?" When you get to your destination take time to write down your observations. Repeat the exercise a second time and compare your notes. This may sound simple, but experts say you can train your mind to be more observant through such simple exercises. A line in an old movie has Sherlock Holmes talking to Dr. Watson where he says, "You see, but you do not observe." It is the Sherlock Holmes type of observation, making note of what you see, that will make you a better angler.

Captain Sutton says you have to pay attention to all your surroundings. "Go to school on anything that changes the surface of the water. Look for movement below the surface, behind a rock, or under a bridge in the shadows." Observing any movement out of the ordinary could put you on some fish. He says to study any wakes as they move and identify the direction of movement. "Study any fish, even a shark, as it makes a head wake, and determine how far out in front of the wake the fish actually is." Being able to determine the fish's position, in relation to the wake, is the most important element of making the right cast to lead the fish properly. A friend of mine once told me he has thought of making a recording that says, "You're behind it," so he could just push a button and not have to say it so many times during the day.

Capt. John Bunch feels the same way about being on the lookout for anything out of the ordinary occurring on the water. His advice is to relax, be patient, and observe what's going on around you. To observe effectively, he suggests just slowing down. In his words, "It takes me sixty-five minutes to watch *60 Minutes* on television, that's my secret. I love to watch the water. Few things on the water ever escape me." While the watching is essential, it's the use of those observations that make you a better angler. Relevant observations include the location of the bait, the stage of the tide, the weather conditions, etc. When those same conditions arise again, the observant angler will have a pretty good idea how to fish them.

The most effective learning through observation will come while on the water. Captain Merrily says, "We have to be more observant if we want to be better anglers." She is quick to point out that she does not mean observing other peoples' fishing spots and stealing them. "Anglers need to go out on the water without a rod on the boat. This forces us to be observers." She says the day will come when you might wish you'd brought your rod because of all the fish you see, but that is not your objective.

Don't be tempted to take the rod; stick to your plan and be an observer. Her routine includes motoring out to a flat that you suspect holds fish. "This may be an area where you've caught fish before, but not that many or not that large. Stay in the area all day, through a full tide cycle if you can. Start right at dawn if possible, or better yet go early and be set up at dawn to see what first light does to the area." If you work during the day, she suggests going after work and staying until dark. Anchor up, and be as quiet as possible as you observe what happens when other boats approach, as baitfish come through the area, as a dolphin appears, or any other event affects life on the flat. You can also use visualization techniques to practice your casts in your head as you observe what the fish are doing. The next time you visit the flat for observation purposes try drifting and compare the fish behavior with a moving boat, as opposed to one that is staked out.

This notion of observation is summed up well by Captain McCue. "I have always been a firm believer that great fishermen and top guides have some of the same characteristics in that they are keen observers, constantly seeing things most others don't, and then they remember them," he says. That's right, remember your observations, and put them to use when the opportunity arises.

Stealth

Especially in shallow water fishing, a stealthy approach to your predator fish is highly desirable. Stealth is defined as acting in a way as to conceal your presence. The notion is really pretty simple, but concealing your presence is not easily carried out on the water. It is a well-known fact that sound carries very well and for longer distances under water. The fish that we pursue have evolved to take advantage of this characteristic and are easily spooked by a noisy angler. Opening a storage hatch, banging the lid on the livewell, or jumping down into the bottom of the boat all send sound waves emanating outward from the boat and warning your prey of your presence. Like any other element of fishing, practice can improve your stealth.

Your practice should be aimed at learning to be quiet when moving around the boat. Practice opening and closing your hatches without banging them, and step quietly when changing positions. Captain Wiggins makes a mental note to practice these simple tasks over and over again. He says, "I move around the boat without rocking it or making noise. I don't recommend this for others, but I will actually close my eyes and move around the boat, remembering where every hatch and step is located. I also have learned where to step in the boat without stepping on creaky hatches." In pre-tournament fishing, or when recreational fishing, Captain Wiggins will pass up a cast on a fish just to see how close he can get and determine how much noise he can make, without spooking the fish. The whole scenario has to be set in relation to existing conditions. He says, "Note the conditions of the water, wind, clouds, boat traffic, or other characteristics. Learning the fish's tolerance to noise will help in tournament or recreational fishing situations, and improve your overall catch ratio."

Given the importance of matching your equipment to the fish that you catch, Captain Wiggins suggests practicing the quiet exchange of one rod for another when required by the size of the fish that you spot. You might also want to pick up a rod with a different lure because of the species of fish that you see. When you need a different rod than the one you are holding, you need to make the exchange without making sounds that spook the fish. There is nothing like a sighted fish to start the adrenaline flowing, but your response needs to be planned, deliberate, and quiet. Chances are, you will do it more quietly if you have practiced the routine before you actually have to perform it.

Trailer Backing, Boat Launching, and Boat Loading

If you fish from a boat and you trailer that boat to different locations, you need to practice backing the trailer, unloading the boat, and loading the boat under different ramp conditions. You also need to develop a certain level of ramp etiquette.

Captain Burns has a saying he uses with respect to trailering a boat and unloading at a ramp. He says, "Be a champ at the ramp." He advises anglers to have all their ducks in a row, be prepared and ready when loading or unloading. When launching the boat, have your drain plug in and necessities such as dock lines, tackle, rods, coolers, etc., loaded ahead of launch time, even if you have to stop and pull off the road before you get to the ramp. That way, when you're ready to back down the ramp and launch, you can be out of the way in the least amount of time for the next guy. After loading the boat back on the trailer and pulling out, stage your boat well away from the ramp area so you won't interfere with someone else needing to use the ramp.

Trailer Backing

Learning to back your trailer is especially important when you first purchase a boat. I've seen the comedy of errors that happens too often at the ramp when the weekend warriors show up to launch. Backing a trailer is not a naturally acquired skill. You have to practice. The best place to do it is in an abandoned parking lot with lots of room to maneuver. If you can find one with painted stripes for the parking spaces, they can be used to measure your success. A couple of cardboard boxes can also be used to set up a practice area.

The reason that backing is difficult for many people is that the trailer will go in the opposite direction of the tow vehicle when backed. However, an easy method of backing can be learned where you use the rear- and side-view mirrors, instead of turning around and looking out the back to see where the trailer is going.

Using this method you simply put the forefinger of your right hand on the bottom of the steering wheel and view the trailer in the side-view mirror. Then simply point your finger in the direction you want the trailer to go as you view it in the mirror. Rotate the steering wheel in the direction your finger is pointing and the trailer will move in that direction. It sounds simple and it really is, but you still must practice to perfect the backing maneuver so that you place the trailer in the water where you want it.

This is where the parking lot and the cardboard boxes come in. Practice in the lot until you are comfortable with the procedure, and then go try it at the ramp. I also suggest you pick an off time, a weekday if possible, so the ramp is not congested enough to add pressure to your backing experience. Remember, you are intentionally practicing your backing maneuver, so don't just back down and launch the boat. Back it in the water and then drive it out. Repeat the procedure for another practice run. Repetition is what will make you a "champ at the ramp."

Keep in mind that the length of the trailer has a big impact on how any given trailer will back. So, don't expect your buddy's boat to back exactly like yours. Shorter trailers may jackknife if you try to back them the same as you would a long trailer. Just take your time and watch what happens in the side-view and rear-view mirrors.

Launching the Boat

You should become completely familiar with your trailer and any devices that secure the boat in place on the trailer. Some ramps will have signs indicating a staging area, but if not designated, use common sense and stage the boat where it is not interfering with another boater's use of the ramp. Load anything you plan to take with you from the car to the boat. Remove all tie-down devices, motor supports, and safety chains, except for the winch strap. Secure a bow

Weekend congestion at boat ramps is common. Be prepared to clear the ramp as quickly as you can to make room for other boaters.

line and a stern line to the boat for use in tying the boat to the dock once you are floating in the water.

Make sure your plug is in the boat. Line up the trailer with the ramp, and back it carefully into the water. When you use a new ramp, ask someone about its condition and if there are any hazards to avoid. Sometimes the ramps are short, and you have to be careful not to drop your tires off the end of the ramp. There can also be underwater obstacles, including hidden rocks or holes. Local knowledge may be needed.

All boats float off the trailer at different positions, so make a mental note of where your trailer fenders are in relation to the water when the boat begins to float and pull away from the bow roller. Making this notation will help you the next time you launch. If you have help, one or two persons can hold the lines as the boat floats off the trailer. If you don't have help, tie the bowline to the trailer and back into the water until the boat floats. Set the parking brake, remove the line from the trailer, and tie the boat to the dock. Once the boat is secured, return to the tow vehicle and pull the trailer out of the water and head to a parking spot.

If you have another experienced driver, the boat can be launched without ropes. This is the best and most convenient situation of all. One person drives the tow vehicle, and the other drives the boat off the trailer and waits in open water. Once the vehicle is parked, the boat can be driven close enough to the dock to be boarded and you are on your way. Always be mindful of other boaters, and clear the ramp as soon as possible so others may use it.

Loading the Boat

Loading the boat back onto the trailer is essentially the opposite of launching it. You must first motor slowly up to the dock and secure the boat to the dock with lines. Retrieve the tow vehicle and back the trailer into the water. Practice will dictate how far to place the trailer into the water. Remember where the fenders were, in relation to the water, when the boat started to float off the trailer when you first launched, and leave them higher when you load.

With the trailer in position, return to the boat; untie the lines and motor up to the trailer. Most trailers have guides that will assist you in lining the boat up and positioning it on the trailer. Use the boat's engine to drive the boat forward to the bow roller, or hook the winch strap to the boat and winch the boat until the bow sits firmly on the roller. Trim the engine to its towing position, replace the safety chain on the bow hook, and pull the boat and trailer to an area where you can complete the process without impeding other boaters from using the ramp. Especially on weekends, boat ramps can be very busy and a little simple courtesy goes a long way in making everyone's boating and fishing experience better.

Once an appropriate parking place has been found, replace all tie downs and engine supports, and reload your vehicle with the personal items you want removed from your boat. Be sure your hitch is secure and your trailer lights are working. It is a good idea to have spare light bulbs and fuses available just in case they are needed. A little pre-planning can help avoid a costly traffic ticket for defective brake lights or turn signals. Drive home, or to the nearest carwash, and clean the boat before storing it. Saltwater will take a toll, especially on metal parts, and the sooner you remove salt spray and residue from your boat and trailer, the better.

Last Cast

When you were in school, you couldn't copy other people's work because it was plagiarism. In fishing, it is actually a good idea to copy other people's stuff, especially when the other people are successful anglers. Not only do you want to copy their success, you want to perfect it. Good anglers willingly develop a strategy to practice their skills in an organized and meaningful manner.

Captain McCue believes practice contributes to confidence in your own fishing abilities. He suggests that, "Fishing is 99 percent confidence. If you've done the preparation and know how to apply your skills, with trust in your gear, your maintenance program, and strategic abilities, you set out with a focused sense of confidence with minimal distractions." The result can only be positive. Improve your confidence by making practice a part of your overall fishing strategy, not just something to do when you can't fish.

5

One if by Land, Two if by Sea

Tips for Fishing from Shore or Boat

It was from the steeple of Christ Church in Boston where the signal would emanate. One lantern in the steeple meant the British were coming by land, two meant the British were coming by sea. Once the signal was sent, the famous ride of Paul Revere marked the beginning of the American Revolution. The British were met and pushed back by the American Minutemen—so named because they could be ready to fight in a minute.

So how does this historic lesson have any connection with a land-based fisherman? Often armed with rod and reel and artificial baits in their vehicle, serious land-based anglers can be fishing in a minute. All that's necessary is a body of water that looks fishy enough to compel you to stop the car or truck and hop out for a few prospecting casts. If you hook up, you stay a while; if not, you go back to whatever you were doing when the fishing urge hit.

For the angler fishing from a boat, it takes a little longer than a minute because of planning, traveling, and launching, but the goal in the end is the same for land-based and boating anglers. Most anglers fish to catch. Some of the techniques used in each type of fishing are the same, although the planning can be different. The time constraint is different too. If you plan to fish from a boat, you need to schedule a little more time than when fishing from land. The minutemen analogy doesn't work for the angler fishing from a boat. Nevertheless, the passion that grips serious fishermen drives them to learn more about the tools, skills, and techniques that will make them better anglers regardless of the fishing platform.

Local Knowledge

There is no substitute for knowledge and experience when it comes to fishing. One of the best things you can do, whether fishing by land or from a boat, is to visit with local anglers and get their tips for fishing in their area. Don't expect secret spots to be revealed, but most anglers will share successful techniques and general information related to the local fishing. They might share with you what bait is working best or the color and type of lure that has been successful. Remember, they gained their local knowledge through experience, by spending time on the water. You too will have to spend the time and pay the price to develop a level of confidence for fishing a particular area. Over time, you might be the person other anglers come to for advice.

Tackle shops and marinas are also excellent sources of local information. The managers of these facilities are in constant contact with anglers and often know where the bite is hot and where it's not. In my experience they have always been a little more willing to name actual locations than individual anglers.

Tackle shops and marinas are excellent sources of local information.

In the high-tech world we live in today, the Internet can be an excellent source of local knowledge. There are many fishing Web sites that provide fishing forums where you can ask and answer serious fishing questions. Quality fishing forums provide a wealth of information from experienced recreational anglers and often include responses from professional fishing guides. An excellent example is the forum hosted by *Florida Sportsman* (www.floridasportsman. com). Other more localized sites are available and easily found by making a quick search on the Web. Tampa Bay, for example is covered well by *Fishing Florida Online Magazine* (www. capmel.com) hosted by Mel Berman. East-central Florida has loads of information on the *Central Florida East Coast Fishing* (www.cfecf.com) site hosted by Gary Craig. Find a site that supports your area, and join the forum to gain more local knowledge. These sites also provide details on tides, weather, and other fishing information that will be important to any angler's success. They may even put you in touch with a fishing buddy to share expenses by fishing together.

In addition to being active on Internet forums, Capt. Tom Van Horn suggests seeking out local fishing clubs and becoming a member. He also suggests reading articles and books and attending fishing seminars where you can ask questions firsthand of expert fishermen. Captain Van Horn adds, "There are many books and publications you can learn from. I still learn from what I read, every day."

Capt. Ron Tomlin, a guide in the Everglades, also believes reading can help you learn about the areas you will fish. He also suggests studying maps and charts of the area before you go fishing as part of your pre-fishing plan. Captain Tomlin says, "I encourage all my folks to study the area where we will be fishing." He even loans them charts to review and tells them what kind of areas to look for. "I also recommend books they can read that will give them information about the species they're after, although the fish don't always read the same books I do. I also suggest that they study what the target fish eats so they have some idea about lure selection."

You should also check out your local radio listings for fishing shows in your area. *Florida Sportsman* hosts radio shows all over the state, and each is filled with knowledge of the local fishing resource. Many local stations host shows manned by charter captains to spread the word to area anglers. These shows operate on a call-in format with listeners asking questions or answering questions from others. These shows are a great way to expand your knowledge of local fisheries.

Fishing Maps

Especially for exploring new fishing areas, fishing maps can cut down on the time needed to isolate the best spots to fish. Any fisherman wants to use time on the water productively. One way to be more productive when fishing is to spend some time with a map before you get on the water. A good fishing map will assist you in finding the points, deep-water boat docks, channel edges, and spoil islands (submerged or visible), as well as numerous other fish attractors. When you stop at the local tackle shop and the proprietor tells you they been biting on the lee side of the spoil islands, a map will lead you to those islands and hopefully to the fish.

The electronic age of the Internet allows anglers to sit in front of their computer and study current fishing areas or search for new

A good fishing map will assist you in finding points, deep-water boat docks, channel edges, and spoil islands (submerged or visible), as well as numerous other fish attractors.

ones. Electronic maps can be purchased for the area you fish or you can use sites such as Teraserver or Google Earth to explore the waters of the world by zooming in, zooming out, and panning. These sites will reveal spoil islands, bottom contours, creeks, and all the various structures important to anglers when seeking their prey.

Begin your study of a fishing map by getting familiar with the various symbols and abbreviations. They are used as a shorthand way of identifying many features that are marked on the map. Symbols will mark fishing areas, diving areas, depth contours, services, parks, boat ramps, navigation aids, and other elements of the map. Abbreviations will identify navigation light characteristics such as color and how long they blink or flash. Abbreviations also identify bottom characteristics such as "Cl" for clay, "Rky" for rocky, or "S" for sand. Learning these symbols and abbreviations will allow you to use your map efficiently in your search for fish.

Once you fish a spot and catch a fish, make note of the geography of the area. Ask yourself questions such as, "Was it a rocky-point or a steep drop off, or does it contain a certain type of cover or structure?" Answering these and other questions will help you find similar spots to fish when the bite cools off. Fish are attracted to certain places for a reason, and once you identify an area that harbors fish you can be pretty sure the fish will congregate in other spots with the same characteristics. Use your map to identify these similar areas.

Good fishing maps have a compass rose imprinted on them. You can use this compass rose to orient the map to the body of water you are fishing. This orientation allows you to identify visible landmarks and coordinate them with the same landmarks on the map. Correspondingly, you can locate underwater structure that is not visible on the map by relating its position with the objects you can identify above the waterline such as bridges, water towers, or canals.

For the land-based angler the maps are useful tools to put fish in the cooler. They can show you underwater creeks and channels that are close enough to cast to from shore. Maps can show you underwater structure and contours that fish are likely to find attractive.

If you are fishing from a boat, using the map along with your sonar can position you in the most likely spot for the fish to be. If you also have a GPS you can mark the spot as a waypoint and easily return to it later. In fact, most quality fishing maps give GPS coordinates that you can program into your system before ever visiting the spot. In this case, when you get the report that the bite is on at Wellman's Creek, all you have to do is navigate to your waypoint and begin fishing. You will also discover your own hotspots that you can mark with an electronic waypoint and also physically pencil the spot in on your map.

Although they usually contain a caution that they are not intended to be used for navigation, maps can help you navigate to your intended destination. The visible structures along the shore, islands, power poles crossing the water, buoys of different types, and many other navigational aids are also marked on the map, giving you an idea of where you are on the water.

Navigating from Islamorada to Flamingo, for example, requires avoiding lots of shallow water, so the route you choose must be followed carefully. A fishing map allows you to visualize the route and also gives you the waypoints to help you complete the trip safely. Just looking at a map will suggest several alternative routes, but if you ask at a local marina, you can probably find the shortest and most navigable route.

Solunar Tables and Tides

Now that you have your trip all mapped out, what are some other factors that might make your fishing adventure more productive? Many anglers rely heavily on the solunar tables available in almanacs, calendars, and other fishing publications to increase their fishing success. The theory identifies four periods each day when the fish are said to be more active. There are two major periods each day and two minor periods. One of each occurs in the a.m. and one of each occurs in the p.m. The major periods last from 2 to 3½ hours and the minor periods last from ¾ to 1½ hours. The tables are based on the relationship of the sun (sol) and moon (lunar) to each other and their position relative to the earth.

Finding the major and minor periods for any day is easy. Many newspapers print them daily, and a quick search of the Internet will provide numerous sites where you can find the information for your area. Capt. Robert McCue has used the solunar tables for years. He says, "There is no question that fish, especially hard-to-catch species such as tarpon and snook, will feed more freely and strike a bait more readily during a major solunar period." He even says that baitfish will become more active and are easier to chum up during a major period. When baitfish are not cooperative, Captain McCue will cast-net enough bait to fish temporarily and come back later during a major period to catch bait for the rest of the day. This way he spends less time in the hunt for bait and more time fishing.

Captain McCue uses the solunar tables to schedule a charter with customers when possible. "When a customer contacts me about a charter and asks me to recommend the best day during a certain month, I check the moon phases and the solunar tables." McCue tries to schedule the trip on a day with a daytime major during a full moon. He believes this scheduling will give him and his customers a good chance at a great fishing day.

Captain McCue adds this advice about solunar periods. "If a major solunar period coincides with a tide change, with sunrise, or sunset—be on your favorite fishing spot when it happens."

Obviously, choosing an exact day to go fishing is a luxury many anglers can't afford. When this is the case, the best day to go is the day you can. Professional fishing guides have this problem often, as clients call and want to go fishing on a particular day. It doesn't really matter what the moon phase or position is; if the client can only go on Tuesday, then Tuesday is the best day to go. The same is true for you. Go when you can go, but use your best information and techniques to make the best of it.

The various stages of the tide determine how fast or how slow the current is running, caused by the flooding and ebbing tides. The flood tide is the incoming or rising tide that occurs between a period of low water and the high water level to follow. The ebb tide is the outgoing or receding flow of water occurring between a period of high water and the lower water to follow.

Many fishing spots are only good during one stage of the tide. Which tide to fish is learned with experience in your own fishing area. As a general rule, Capt. Rick Grassett likes to fish when the tide or current is most active. He says, "Think of the tide as a conveyor belt moving food to the fish." After all, finding the food source is another important part of fishing success.

Capt. Dale Fields adds, "Without a doubt, the most critical factor in fishing is tide. If there is no water movement, the fish don't bite. Water temperature plays a big role also, but water movement is the driving factor in fishing success."

Captain Ed "Jazz" Jazwierski reminds us that tides are also important to gaining access to productive fishing areas. For example, if you venture into the backcountry, you should go on an incoming or flooding tide. "There's nothing worse than not being able to get out until the tide turns. If the no-see-ums are out while you wait, oh boy, you'll lose some blood for sure!"

Transplanted Floridian Capt. Troy Mell adds, "Moving water moves bait. The game fish will follow this bait or wait in ambush points along the current. An incoming tide also allows fish to move up on flats to search for food that they were not able to search for at a low tide." He says the whole scenario will get a little tricky as the moon phase and wind forces affect the tide height. Nevertheless, tide-recording stations are a great place to start gathering information, and they can be found easily on the Internet. Tide charts are normally available in local tackle shops or magazines as well. Captain Troy advises anglers to "explore new areas on an incoming tide—this way you will reduce your risk of getting stuck."

Professional anglers expect the most productive fishing at or near the new and the full moon. Capt. Rick Burns advises, "Fish around the moon phases. Four days before and after new and full moons gives a total of sixteen days that should be more productive than other days in any given month. The gravitational pull during the times closer to these phases creates stronger tides that increase feeding activity." Captain Burns asserts that fishing during these periods will result in more fish caught, on average, than at other times.

Structure and Cover

Whether you find it on your own, learn from a local angler, or pull it off a fishing map, structure and cover are important to fishing success. Fish are attracted to structure and cover for protection, comfort, and as an area that provides food. The term *cover* refers to anything that provides shelter for the fish, as well as the baitfish that our predators seek. Cover would include vegetation or even a man-made dock. Cover provides security to smaller fish and the small fish attract the larger predators anglers are looking for.

Cover is an important part of the aquatic food chain. In scientific terms, the food chain is the transfer of food energy, beginning in plants, from small organisms to larger ones. Each member of the aquatic community eats smaller members, while at the same time being preyed upon by larger members of the community. Mullet eat plants, sea trout eat mullet, snook eat trout, sharks eat snook, and so it goes. Remember, it all began with the cover as a habitat for the smallest of organisms.

Structure is something that is in someway different than the surrounding area. It is a physical characteristic of the terrain. On the Florida grass flats, a pothole (sand spot) in the grass provides an area for redfish, sea trout, and other species to warm their bodies when the water temperatures are cool. These same potholes provide an ambush point where predator fish lurch from the grass to eat a passing baitfish. The sand hole itself is structure, the surrounding grass is cover. Finding both cover and structure together is often the key to fishing success.

Points

One of the simplest fishing structures is a point. A point may be exposed above the waterline or concealed below. When the point is connected to the land above the waterline it is easily detected by land-based anglers or boaters alike. Points can also be submerged and must be identified by maps or sonar equipment. Points will cause certain fish to congregate and feed on the smaller baitfish that are also attracted to the point. Currents running over the point, wind, sunlight, or other environmental factors contribute to the attractiveness of the structure. As mentioned above, structure and cover together multiply the opportunity to find fish.

Capt. Chris Myers guides the grass flats of the legendary Mosquito Lagoon in east-central Florida and fishes all over the state. He views points as natural ambush stations for predators. In areas characterized by tidal flows or in areas with wind-driven current, the water movement over the points can create eddies that trap or disorient baitfish making them easy prey for larger fish. His favorite way to fish a point is to use small artificial baits, such as a D.O.A. shrimp. His advice is to cast upcurrent from the point and reel in just enough line to take out the slack, while letting the lure swim naturally over the point.

An outgoing tide allows an angler to drift bait across a fishy point. Use moving water to your advantage.

Capt. Ron Tomlin does most of his fishing in Everglades National Park. He likes to fish both sides of a point. "I have found that fish will hold on both sides of a wind- or current-swept point. I generally find better action on the lee side." He explains that the lee-side action relates to the ambush tactics of fish. "Either wind or current sweeps bait around a point, whether it's a point of mangroves, a sandbar, or an oyster bar." When that bait sweeps over the point, the predators are lying in wait for the ambush. Captain Tomlin says he often finds larger fish holding farther off the point waiting for an urge to move in and feed. His preferred method for targeting the bigger fish requires staying back off the point and fan-casting across both sides thoroughly. He makes every effort to fish with the wind or current flow, while covering both sides of the point. He says, "My personal love is to pull a topwater bait across the point and enjoy the explosive strike of a hungry fish."

Land-based anglers should approach a point quietly and observe the water on each side. Depending on conditions, the fish may be on one side or the other. If the water is flowing, the fish will probably be downcurrent and facing the point, waiting for bait to be swept toward them. The position of the sun may also affect your success. I have often caught jack crevalle or ladyfish on a point when the sun is high and shining brightly. In low-light conditions, early or late in the day, I have caught spotted sea trout and snook off of the same point. Fish are sensitive to light and the comfort factor of each individual species comes into play in determining when they show up on a point. This fact relates to the age-old adage that fishing is generally better early and late in the day.

Generally, any fish's relation to structure will depend on its comfort and the availability of food. The comfort aspect may be any number of factors, such as water temperature, water clarity, or the amount of daylight. The food factor is the simplest; either there is food or there is not. When baitfish are not present, you are normally better off to keep looking. How different fish relate to points, or any structure for that matter, is knowledge that will come with experience as you spend time on the water and log your successes for future adventures.

Ledges

Another common structure sought out by anglers is a ledge, which occurs where the bottom changes from one depth to another. A ledge can be a steep immediate drop or it may be a more gradual sloping drop. Personally, I have always favored steep drops; they normally produce better results. Ledges provide not only fish-attracting structure, but also a route for fish moving from one location to another. Capt. Keith Kalbfleisch advises anglers to be ever conscious of changing bottom structure. He says, "A six-inch depth change on a flat may be enough to funnel the fish in a different direction—maybe right to you!" Redfish will move from the security of deep water up and over the ledge to feed on the flats where anglers can sightfish for them.

Capt. Rick Burns likes the protected side of a ledge coupled with tidal flow because it holds bait- and game fish, which don't have to exhaust a lot of energy to feed. "The ledge can be a good feeding spot because the food source that is washed over the drop-off can be easy pickings for predator game fish. The fish instinctively know that food is coming with the tide, and they don't have to work hard for a meal. Would you rather somebody bring your meal to you, or go out and work for it every time?"

Other Structure

Other types of structure include cuts, humps, and holes. A cut is an indentation in the bottom that provides water that is deeper in the cut than the shallow water around it. A hump is a structure that rises from the bottom with deep water all around it and shallow water on top. A small underwater island is a hump. Fish can swim all the way around a hump in deeper water for security and comfort and move up on the hump in search of baitfish when they are hungry. Depending on conditions and the tidal stage, the bite can be good at any of the various depths associated with the hump. When prospecting around a hump, you should be sure to fish all the way down the water column.

A hole is the opposite of a hump. This structure contains a bowl of deep water surrounded by shallow water. Fish it similar to a hump; cover all the various water depths from the edge of the hole to the bottom.

Captain Burns fishes the Homosassa and Crystal River area of Florida's West Coast. Specializing in light-tackle and fly fishing, he loves to fish points but also searches out little coves or pockets that may hold fish. He says, "These structures may be no bigger than your kitchen table, just something that is different or out of the norm of the surrounding area." They may be a small depression hole or deeper area, a calmer area, or maybe just dead wood lying in the water that provides protection or comfort to the fish. Captain Burns says, "I've experienced this too many times; fish will concentrate and can be caught out of these surprisingly small spots."

Captain Burns says he doesn't try to distinguish between structure and cover. He says the difference is hard to distinguish and there is really no reason to. He argues, "A house is a structure, but it can also be cover. A log or submerged tree limb or mangrove roots can be structure, but they definitely provide cover. Just ask a snook!"

As you can see, there are many types of structure including combinations of those discussed above. Anytime you get a change in the physical characteristics of the bottom you have found structure. When you find structure that produces fish, mark it on your map or as a waypoint on your GPS. You will definitely want to return in the future.

Maybe Captain Jazz says it best. When asked to name his favorite type structure, "My favorite is the structure with the fish on it. I don't really discriminate. I fish it all."

Captain Jazz says tidal flow or current is also an important element of fishing structure. He normally fishes structure in one of two ways. Fish from the front of the structure, such as a dock, by feeding live bait back under the structure. Or, fish perpendicular to the structure and cast upcurrent, letting your offering sweep by with the current. "Both ways will work, and you'll feel the take better. Keep slack in your line to a minimum. You always want to 'feel' what your bait is doing. It could be snagged on the bottom, may have caught a mangrove root, hooked on an oyster bar, or best of all, been taken by a fish. You'll never know with slack in the line."

Water temperature will impact the congregation of fish on any given structure. Once again, this is the comfort element at work. When the water temperatures drop, fish move to their comfort level. If you caught fish on the top of a hump when the surface temperature was 78, you are more likely to find them deeper along the hump when the surface temperature is 65. The same thing is true on a shallow flat, except that during the winter the flat will warm quickly on a sunny day. The fish will return, but it will be later in the day. You have to plan you trip accordingly. Many master anglers plan their wintertime flats trips for later in the day after the sun has warmed the water. Hey, it's a chance to sleep in and still have a great day on the water.

Man-Made Structure

In addition to all the natural structure, there are many man-made structures as well. Nearshore and offshore waters are filled with various artificial structures that attract fish. Fishing clubs and other organizations often team up with government agencies to build artificial reefs that can be identified on maps and set as waypoints on your GPS. Everything from naval vessels to concrete balls have been use to create artificial fish attractors. If you are lucky enough to have one in your area, it would certainly be worthy of a cast or two to determine if it holds any fish.

Weather

Neither rain, nor sleet, nor snow, nor wind, nor dead of night shall deter the serious fisherman from his appointed rounds. It's true that anglers have a capacity and tolerance for fishing in the worst weather. Sometimes, anglers hit the water despite the weather be-

Bad weather did not stop this angler from engaging in a day of fishing, but always think safety first.

cause it's simply the only time they have to go, and sometimes they just got caught unprepared. Weather should be a factor in planning any fishing trip. Most master anglers will tell you that the weather is one of the things they always look at the day before a trip.

Capt. Pat Dineen describes just how weather can influence your fishing location as well as the fish you target. Captain Dineen is a professional fishing guide and the Northwest Region Reporter on the *Chevy Florida Fishing Report* seen on Sunsports TV. He explains how wind speed and direction can hugely affect the tidal movement and magnitude in the backwaters he fishes. Some local areas where he catches redfish most of the year may actually be dry during the winter because of the strong and blustery northerly winds. When the southerly summer breezes return, water gets pushed back into the backcountry, giving fishermen two feet or more of water in areas that had been unfishable.

Weather is also extremely important when heading out to open waters where you often travel for miles to reach a fishing destination. Being aware of the weather allows you to plan the direction and distance you wish to travel and will help you make the day as much fun as possible. Captain Dineen gives an example. Say you start the day out with the prediction of strong westerly or southwesterly winds for later in the day. Throughout the day, you'll want to plot your route so that you are returning to port with these winds at your back and not at your face. You must plan your day according to the best information you have available. Captain Dineen says, "It's no fun to be way out east and have to pound your way home into a sloppy and nasty head sea!" The weatherman is not always right, but he is a source of generally good information, and you should use it to your advantage.

Don't forget that weather will affect not only the fishing, but also the availability of bait. For anglers depending on live bait, changing weather may make your bait totally unavailable or more plentiful. If you need to catch bait, you would be wise to keep records of where and when you were able to find that bait during specific conditions. These records can be just as important to your knowledge base as any other component. Without your preferred bait, you have to turn to plan B—which might mean changing your targeted fish or buying bait before you leave the dock.

When planning his charters, Captain Jazz likes to look at wind direction and what the tide is "supposed" to do. He uses the word "supposed" because the wind can play a major role in what the tides actually do. He fishes Tampa Bay (on Florida's West Coast) and explains that a strong northeasterly can actually hold up or kill an incoming tide. A strong wind can retard the water from moving up into the bay, which results in no or little water on the flats, leaving concentrations of fish in smaller areas. He says, "This can be great for fishing, but not so good on engine lower units."

The opposite could be true with a southwesterly wind. Then, tides can be higher than predicted and the fish will be spread out over a larger area—even in areas where they normally would not be. Captain Jazz adds this word of warning associated with tides that are higher than predicted, "Some things may be submerged that are normally visible, and there can also be an increase in floating debris that causes a hazard to boating."

Although weather forecasts are just that, forecasts or expectations, they at least provide some information that anglers should take into account before putting themselves in harm's way. It is bad enough that the inclement weather can ruin a fishing trip, but you certainly do not want to put your health and safety—and someone else's—at risk for the mere joy of catching a fish. With good health, there will always be another fishing trip. So first, consider the weather as a safety factor, and if the weather is expected to be too bad, just don't go.

Sometimes, the decision to go or not to go is easier than at other times. It's no secret; Florida is the lightning capital of the world. If you are unloading your boat in a lightning storm, you should reconsider. If you are looking at a forecast of afternoon storms, as is often the case with Florida summers, go ahead and go fishing, but keep your eye on the sky and get back to the dock before they hit. When the weather turns nasty, it can be very destructive. Captain Burns says, "I usually let clients know there are too many good days in

Florida to take a chance on a bad one. After all, half the experience is enjoying the day."

Captain Jazz, along with most master anglers, identifies lightning as the element of the weather to fear the most, and he has some good advice about thunderstorms. "Be smart and don't risk your life for a few fish, or worse yet, risk the life of a friend or family member. It's just not worth it. If you are driving the vessel, it's your responsibility to return your passengers safely to the dock. Stay close to your ramp and fish nearby; if the weather does start to get nasty, it's a very short ride to safe harbor."

Capt. Ron Tomlin does much of his fishing in the Everglades, often for extended periods of time. Some of his charters are multi-day camping-and-fishing trips. Planning to be away from civilization for more than a day requires special attention to the forecast. Captain Ron watches the weather carefully before a trip, especially watching out for thunderstorms and lightning. He says lightning is the worst element of weather. "It's totally unpredictable and can do the most damage. If the weather forecast is severe, I may suggest canceling a charter, but generally, I will go and just watch the weather carefully." He says he doesn't mind getting wet, but he wants to get everyone back safely, and the only way to do it is to keep track of any severe weather conditions. He catches as many fish in the rain as when it's not raining and sometimes more. "Rain is more of a fisherman hindrance than a fishing hindrance. I think the infusion of cold aerated rain water is good for the receiving waters and activates the fish."

Captain McCue is also willing to fish in inclement weather. "Short of a hurricane, depression, or some very significant adverse weather prediction, I no longer cancel trips based on the weather forecast. I show up at the dock and make that call on the spot. I have learned many times, the forecasts can be wrong." He goes on to explain that he has fished in more adverse weather than he cares to remember, but the experience gained from these outings has made him a better angler. "I always tell others that professional guides are not always the best fishermen. In fact they rarely are. What they are is consistent. They consistently catch fish under nearly any weather conditions."

As for how the weather affects fishing, there are several elements that deserve consideration. The most important among them are probably wind and barometric pressure. Others include clouds, air temperature, and fronts. And they all are related in one way or another.

Wind

As an angler, you will have to learn to deal with the wind. I basically dislike high winds when fishing—not because the fish won't bite, but because it normally makes for a less desirable experience. Captain Van Horn says, "As far as the fish are concerned, the wind doesn't blow underwater, but locating them and staying on them becomes an extreme challenge."

If you check the weather forecast and find a prediction of high winds for your next expedition, get out your map and study it in relation to which way the winds will blow. Pick an area where you can possibly hide from the wind and use it to your advantage. Remember the discussion on fishing points? Fish tend to lie on the lee side of the points waiting for the baitfish to be swept their way. Residential canals can also be a great place to hide from the wind and still have a good day of fishing.

Captain Van Horn says that if the winds are bad enough, you just may want to reschedule your trip. "I like to enjoy my day on the water, and I like for my clients to have a memorable experience. So, if the winds are greater than fifteen knots I give them the option to cancel. I also feel it is prudent to cancel a charter if a small-craft warning is issued. No fishing trip is worth an injury or losing a boat, so I refuse to venture out into a storm for the sake of profit or fun."

Casting in the wind is an art in itself. If you are drifting a flat, you don't have much choice which way you go. When it's blowing thirty miles an hour you can get really long casts, but by the time you take up the slack you are probably right over your bait and you have covered very little territory. You can try to use the trolling motor to slow your drift, but that takes away from your stealthy approach. Another good alternative is a drift sock, which will slow you considerably and allow a more efficient coverage of the area being fished.

When casting from point A to point B you may have to aim at point C to allow for a strong wind. It takes a lot of patience and practice to make good accurate casts in the wind. Another big problem with the wind is that it blows an arc in your line. Even the most-seasoned veterans of the water admit that you have to pay close attention to the slack caused by wind in order to maintain contact with your bait and be ready for the strike.

In order to lessen the bow caused by the wind, you need to make line-drive casts low to the water. This method will minimize bow in the line and give you a quicker connection to your bait and any potential strike. To keep the line straight, stop the line before the bait hits the water. This will let the weight of the bait pull the line tight before it drops to the waiting prey. You can stop the spool by closing the bail or using your index finger on a spinning outfit or stop the spool with your thumb on a bait caster. Of course, casting with the wind or straight against it will also lessen the amount of bow created in the cast.

In reality, you just need to learn to work with the wind. Don't consider it an adversary, because you will encounter it often and you must try to use it to your advantage. Remember, just because it's windy does not mean the fish won't bite. In fact, if other conditions such as a major feeding period exist, they just may bite better.

Barometric Pressure

I have a friend who wears a barometer around his neck. Why? Because he is convinced, along with a lot of other anglers, that fish are highly affected by barometric pressure. Scientists tell us that if the barometer indicates a decrease in atmospheric pressure, we can expect deteriorating weather and the possibility of rain. If the barometer is rising, we can expect fair weather and sunny skies. The use of barometric pressure is not new as a way to predict the weather or as an element of predicting fish-feeding tendencies. Fishermen have, over time, developed certain expectations in the way fish behave according to the atmospheric pressure. Captain Van Horn outlines one expectation when he says, "High pressure, northeasterly wind, and a full moon equal no fish on the flats."

Without going deeply into the science, the barometric pressure changes as the weather above us changes. To understand how the pressure affects fishing, we need to consider high, normal, and low pressure. Considering 30 inches of mercury (inHG) as normal, anything above 30 inches is high and anything below 30 is low. When you see a blue "H" and a red "L" on a weather map, they are indicating areas of high pressure and areas of low pressure. The normal range of movement will vary from a low of about 28.5 to a high of about 30.5. Remember, normal is at 30 inches of mercury.

If you have the luxury to fish anytime you want, you would wait until the barometer has been at a normal level and is falling. This is when master anglers say the bite will be the best. Even a fall of a few hundredths can produce an improved and aggressive bite. As the barometer falls more, the fish remain active, but not as much as when it first began to fall. Remember, the falling barometer is an indication of deteriorating weather and increases the chances that clouds may soon set in. As the barometer continues to fall and remains low, the fish become less active and the bite may taper off.

Beyond the safety factor related to bad weather, Captain Tomlin considers barometric pressure to have a major impact on fishing success. He follows the school of thought that says any changing barometer is conducive to good fishing. His personal choice would be a dropping barometer. "If I can be on the water ahead of a low front and during the front, it is usually great fishing. For a couple of days after the front, I really have to work much harder to find fish." Most master anglers agree that if the barometer is steady, finding and catching fish will be tougher. Fish a changing barometer when you can.

Starting at a normal of 30 inches, a rising barometer can also improve the bite at first. As the pressure continues to rise to a higher level, the bite once again slows and fish tend to seek deeper water. The highs and the lows tend to cause fish to become less active. Either rising or falling pressure is better than steady pressure, as long as it is neither very high nor very low. Table 3 outlines various weather patterns, fish activity, and fishing strategies to use under different pressure conditions.

Table 3. Barometric Pressure and Fishing

Pressure Trend	Typical Weather	Fishing Trends	Suggested Tactic
High	Clear	Fish activity slows down. Fish seek cover or go to deeper water.	Slow down presentation. Fish in cover and deeper water.
Rising	Clearing or improving	Fish tend to be slightly more active.	Fish with brighter lures and near cover. Fish at intermediate and deeper depths.
Normal and Stable	Fair	Normal fishing	Experiment with your favorite baits and lures.
Falling	Degrading	Most active fishing time.	Speed up lures. Surface- and shallow-running lures may work well.
Slightly Lower	Usually Cloudy	Many fish will leave cover and seek shallow waters. Some fish become more aggressive.	Use shallow-running lures at moderate speed.
Low	Rainy and Stormy	Fish will tend to become less active the longer this period lasts.	As the action subsides, try fishing at deeper depths.

Source: Lee Adams, Effects of Barometric Pressure on Fishing, Tim's Fish Pages. <www.quickoneplus.com/fish/articles>, accessed July 13, 2007.

Captain Jazz also prefers the barometer to be rising or falling. "I like it moving up or falling, but not bottomed out. High pressure can really curtail the bite. You may see a lot of fish laid up, but they don't chew too well. That's when you try to get an anger strike." When the fish aren't hungry, they might bite out of anger, which is basically the fish's way of defending its turf. "An anger strike is when a fish strikes something not because it's hungry, but because he is bothered; it's a territorial sort of thing. Say you see a fish laying in a couple feet of water and you throw the bait near it, but the fish doesn't even move. Sometimes, if you keep repeating the cast over and over, the fish may strike at the bait to get it out of its face. The fish will get tired of seeing the same bait over and over, invading its space, making it angry, and it may strike at it."

Captain Jazz suggests that while you are making these repeated casts, it's important to keep the bait as close to the fish as possible but not to line or touch the fish with the bait. That will spook it and often move it to another area. With respect to snook, he adds this caveat. "I don't do this to laid-up snook when the water temp is below sixty degrees. At this temperature the snook is fighting for survival and is already stressed from the cold, so I leave them alone."

Other Weather Factors

Other weather factors that can affect your fishing include clouds, air temperature, and fronts. As you can tell by the previous discussion, all weather is related in one way or another. As low-pressure areas approach, the barometer is falling and the weather deteriorates. This low-pressure area brings clouds that can have a major impact on an angler's ability to sight fish.

Air temperature is transferred to the water, and when the air temperatures fall, water temperatures will not be far behind. Cooler water temperatures tend to drive fish to deeper water in search of their comfort level. Table 4 indicates a lower comfort level, an ideal comfort level, and an upper comfort level for selected saltwater fish. Knowing these temperature ranges can help you plan your trip around a species that is most likely to be active during a specific range of water temperatures.

Table 4. Temperature Ranges For Saltwater Fish

Species	Lower Temp Limit	Ideal Temp Limit	Upper Temp Limit
Black Drum	52	72	90
Bluefish	50	66–72	82
Bonefish	60	72–84	92+
Cobia	65	75	88
Flounder (Winter)	36	50	64
Flounder (Summer)	56	62–66	72
Jack Crevalle	70	75–85	90
King Mackerel	65	68–76	88
Permit	70	75–85	92
Pompano	65	70–82	85+
Redfish	52	70–90	90+
Sheepshead	58	66	74
Snook	60	70–82	90
Spanish Mackerel	68	78	88
Spotted Sea Trout	48	68–78	88
Tarpon	70	75–90	100+

Source: Central Florida East Coast Fishing <http://home.cfl.rr.com/floridafishing/temp.htm>, accessed January 7, 2008.

Note: This table is a rough guide of desired temperatures for the listed species. By using this guide you can possibly avoid targeting certain species when the water temperatures are not in the range that the species likes. Other variances such as high oxygenated surface areas or schools of baitfish will cause feeding outside the limits.

In the winter, when water temperatures fall, many master anglers advise sleeping in and letting Mother Nature warm the water with her brilliant rays of winter sunshine before the fishing begins. A temperature rise of only a few degrees can make the difference between a successful day and getting skunked. Shallow-water flats, devoid of redfish in the early morning, can be teeming with fish later in the day, after the sun has warmed the water to their preferred temperature.

Scientists tell us that cold water slows the metabolism of fish, and when that happens, fish eat only about one-fourth the amount of food they eat in the summer. Also, the fish will not expend a lot of energy to chase down a meal. So when cold conditions have set in, most pros will tell you to slow down your presentation and retrieve.

If you continue to retrieve your presentations in a quick fashion, as you would in summer, you may be moving the bait right by the fish before they have a chance to strike.

Fishing Logbooks

You can enter information such as weather, water temperature, barometric pressure, moon, tide, etc.—anything you think may help you catch more fish in the future—in a logbook. Captain Myers has logs dating back to the early 1990s. He includes not only his own catch information, but also notes from other anglers who have had good luck catching fish around certain dates. "The biggest thing a complete log does," he says, "is to give me places to look for fish at certain times of the year that I may have forgotten about. It also helps me know when to start looking in places that I might fish only certain times of the year."

Captain McCue is also a believer in logging your fishing activity. "I think a logbook is a good starting point for any angler but particularly a new one. Key information such as tides, water and air temperatures, areas fished, species caught, wind speed and direction, and general barometric pressures start to build a blueprint for patterning fish." It is not really a secret that being able to pattern fish is truly one of the key components for successful anglers.

Fishing conditions change every day, and you have to factor in all the variables that particular day throws at you. Captain McCue says, "With a solid logbook, developing strategies on past, or historic results is a key component in designing a fishing strategy that will work." As your time on the water increases and your fishing information has been systematically logged, you finally reach a point where it is not as important as when you first began keeping the log. Captain McCue says, "I no longer keep logs or plan a strategy the night or day before. I usually do that mentally in the morning with real-time decisions, because my logs are stored in my head." This last statement is the proof in the pudding that logs actually help you become a better angler. The log can be looked at as one of the tools you use to add to your fishing knowledge.

For some master anglers, knowing the historical location of bait is just as important as knowing where the fish can be found. Snook specialist Capt. Danny Guarino says, "For anyone who uses live bait and catches their own, they need to know where the bait may be located and what the weather conditions are that might influence finding it." By referring to historical data, Captain Guarino will at least have a good idea of where to start his search for bait. "It's not an exact science, but the history will help me decide where I will start my search!"

Logs might actually be more helpful for anglers who do not get on the water very often. These occasional fishers can benefit from information in the log, which will help them find some fish. Professional guides are on the water on a regular basis, and that constant presence on the water makes it easier for guides to keep up with the location of fish.

Shore-Bound Anglers

The information covered to this point in the chapter will help anyone catch more fish, be it from a boat on the water or a lawn chair on the land. But now, let's consider a few tips that apply specifically to the shore-bound angler. The following tips should be considered in relation to all the previously mentioned techniques that have an impact on fishing success.

As stated before, the time allotted to fishing is improved when you fish from shore, instead of a boat. Boating anglers have to hook up and tow the boat, unload it at the ramp, and launch—it takes some real time. In my experience, it is even more likely that when you come back to the ramp there will be a little additional wait time to get the boat back on the trailer. Since the saltwater environment will play havoc with trailers, brakes, and anything metal, you will need to spend another hour or so after you return from the fishing trip to clean and unload the boat. This maintenance time is fishing time for shore-bound anglers.

The number-one piece of advice given by Florida master anglers to shore-bound anglers is to move around to different areas in order to find the bite. Many shore anglers have a favorite place to go, and they fish it time after time. Sometimes the fishing is great, but other times it's not. The reason is simple. Fish move around and the angler should move around also. If the area you are fishing is large enough to move up and down the shore until you catch a fish, that is exactly what you should do.

Shore anglers can use artificial lures as prospecting baits. Walk up and down the shore line looking for "fishy" spots and cast to them. Artificial lures allow you to cover a lot more water and possibly find fish quicker than casting out bait and waiting for a fish to come along. Once the prospecting pays off and you catch a fish, then you should concentrate on that area until the bite subsides. When the bite stops, move again until you find another area that produces fish. This may mean getting in your car and moving to a completely different area, but if you want to improve your success, you need to do it.

The shore-bound angler should use a map (as discussed above) to find those areas of structure and cover that are close enough to be reached from shore. Easy fishing access can be found around bridges, city, and county parks with piers, or even the seashore. If you like to fish at night, many of these structures have lights that add an additional fish attractor to the equation. Your own comfort will also be improved by fishing during the cool nights instead of the often-hot Florida days.

Fish are not naturally tolerant to sunlight, and they seek shade for comfort. Fish any area that provides shade, and you will increase your chances for a hook up. Overhanging trees, boat docks, piers, buoys, or other floating objects provide shade and should be fished thoroughly. Also, look for flowing water that may be found at culverts immediately following a rain shower. The intersection of a small stream with a river is also a good place to fish.

Shore-bound anglers can also hit the water and wade. Wade-fishing can be a very productive way to chase down some of Florida's feisty game fish. The great advantage of wading is the stealthy approach that you gain. In fact, most master anglers agree, you can get closer to fish by wading than you can in a boat—some anglers even

Fishing piers (*far background*), jetties (*middle*), and beaches (*foreground*) all provide excellent fishing platforms for shore-bound anglers. Visit with the regulars to get tips on local fishing conditions.

get out of their boat to approach spooky fish. There is an old saying that if you can see the fish, the fish can see you. The profile of a wading or crouching angler presents a much lower profile than the bottom of an angler's boat with a guide standing on a poling platform. This advantage of stealth can pay big dividends in the catching department.

Although boats carry anglers to areas that might be inaccessible to wade fishermen, the opposite is also true. The skinniest water on the planet is accessible by an angler who is wading. If you have areas where you fish and you can visit them at low tide, it can reveal the wonders that lay submerged when the tide comes in. Look for the holes, humps, bumps, and ridges and fish them when you return. You need to know the area you are going to fish. If you don't have tides, fish slowly and move deliberately to learn the area as you fish.

Capt. Merrily Dunn guides in southwestern Florida and fishes the redfish-tournament trail but still has time for a little wade-fishing.

She often gives advice to her clients who want to hang around and fish from shore or wade—after their charter with her. Her number-one piece of advice is to get a local street map and use it to drive around the area and find access points where you can legally get to the water. She says, "Always obey the local laws, or when you return from fishing you might be walking home!"

Once the access has been found and if you are unfamiliar with the fishing grounds, she believes that you should go at low tide. This way you will be better able to tell what the bottom structure is like. She says, "Deep holes will be easier to find and sandbars will be exposed to identify walking paths." Many saltwater fish will move up into these shallow areas with the rise of the tide, and the fish will find those holes on the fall of the tide. She also recommends winter as a great time to go wade-fishing because the tides are generally much lower than in the spring and summer.

As far as equipment is concerned, Captain Merrily says to keep it simple. She suggests getting one of the many great functional wading caddies that are available on the market. These caddies can carry a soft cooler for drinks (she freezes bottled water to carry in the caddy), places for tackle boxes, and even an extra rod. Instead of attaching a fish stringer to your body, attach it to the wading caddie and attach the caddie string to your body. Use a small weight to keep the caddie from floating away from you. This method allows you to fish away from the caddy and then walk back to it. "Use enough weight so that fish attached to the caddie won't be able to move it very far." If you prefer using live bait, pick out a caddy with a built-in bait box.

If you do decide to wade, be sure to take the necessary safety precautions. Underwater hazards can cause serious harm. Wade fishermen should wear tennis shoes or specialty wading boots made to protect their feet from sharp objects, such as broken glass or oyster shells. Wading anglers should also use the "stingray shuffle." These creatures are very common in Florida waters, and they lie partially buried in the bottom and are barely visible to the naked eye. Instead of stepping forward as you move through the water, scoot your feet along the bottom without raising them. This procedure will normally flush a stingray out ahead of you before you step on it and feel the penetrating pain of a barb in your foot or leg.

Captain Merrily says, "Stingrays are nothing to laugh at. I've drifted over many while on my boat, and they have a habit of resting with their tail up. Step on one in light tennis shoes and you'll be in pain at the hospital."

Capt. "Bouncer" Smith may be best known for his swordfish exploits or his many offshore tournament victories, but he too has some great advice for the shore-bound angler: Avoid busy time periods. He suggests fishing late in the evening or very early in the morning. "Swimmers, boat wakes crashing against the sea wall or jetty, and jet skis all put fish on alert and turn off the bite." If you are fishing the surf, pick an incoming tide for best results.

Regardless of the fishing environment you need to pack light and think safety. Captain Bouncer recommends packing leaders already cut to length, just a couple of your favorite lures, one rod, and an inflatable life jacket. "Falling from a sea wall or dock, being sucked out by an undertow or trying to reach the other side of a creek or bay can be deadly."

Captain Bouncer advises the shore-bound angler to think before casting. "Don't always cast perpendicular to your position on the shore. Try casting parallel to the shoreline, whether a sea wall, beach, or jetty. The fish are searching your platform for food or shelter. They are often right at your feet."

Last Cast

All this terminology may start to feel a bit overwhelming. Structure, barometric pressure, wind speed, water temperature, and all the other conditions affecting fishing should not interfere with your enjoyment of the sport. Believe me, it will all become second nature to you as you spend time on the water in pursuit of your passion. Your own observations will be among the most valuable assets you have in your arsenal.

Fishing is a recreational sport with more participants than spectators. In fact, there is ever-increasing pressure being put on

Florida's fishery resource by more and more participants. This trend makes understanding the finer points of angling a necessity, especially if you want to achieve a high level of success. This increased fishing pressure makes the fish more wary and harder to catch and gives you one more reason to stay on top of your game. As you engage in your fishing endeavors you will quickly learn that knowledge and skills are more productive than luck. Don't just leave your fish-catching to luck when there are so many avenues available to help you improve your odds.

Wanted Dead or Alive

Fishing with Natural Baits

All fishing trips start out with high expectations and excitement for the fishing experience to come. For live-bait fishermen, the day often starts in search for bait that will be used that day. I can remember many times when that search lasted entirely too long, but other times, when the search ended happily and quickly.

Once, on a trip out of Port Canaveral, a couple friends and I encountered flipping pogies (Atlantic menhaden) before we left the port. A couple throws of the cast net were all that were necessary to secure the needed bait. With bait in hand, we headed into nearshore waters, where we spotted a bait pod being attacked by hungry fish. Two out of the three anglers quickly hooked up with a feisty bonito, and a promising day of fishing was underway. Later we found an area where rolling tarpon captured our attention, and sure enough it didn't take long to hook up. The tarpon won, as they often do, but because we found the bait early, we were able to hunt for game fish more thoroughly, and our quest was successful.

One week later, a similar trip turned out much different. We cruised out of the port without seeing any bait. We traveled southward, watching for diving birds to signal the presence of baitfish. No birds, no bait, and by the end of the day, no fish. After spending two or three futile hours looking, there was no other choice but to turn to alternatives. When cast-netting fails, other options to get live bait include sabiki rigs, hook and line, or sometimes, you can purchase bait from a local dealer. If attempts to get live bait fail, you can turn to the dead or frozen variety. No matter how anglers get it, natural bait is the most important element of many a fishing trip.

This chapter will identify some of the baitfish most preferred by Florida's master anglers. The discussion will center on inshore species, but many of the same baitfish are used offshore as well. Often, the choice of natural bait depends on the species of game fish you are targeting, and there are many more species of baitfish than will be identified here. You should always check local bait shops and marinas for the popular bait used in the area you intend to fish.

The availability of baitfish is often seasonal, and anglers have to adapt to differing scenarios. If a specific species is seasonal, many master anglers suggest capturing some and putting them in your

A mixture of three parts salt to one part baking soda, mixed in an icy slush, preserves the quality and appearance of frozen baitfish.

freezer when they are abundant, so you will have that bait for the times when they are hard to find. Capt. Tom Van Horn says, "For backup, I always carry a package of frozen mullet. Each year during the mullet run, I will take a day or two to net a couple five-gallon buckets' full of finger mullet and freeze them in sandwich-size bags to use later in the season when there are no mullet around."

If you want to go that extra mile when freezing baitfish, you can soak them in a solution of ground salt and baking soda. Most kitchens already have the needed ingredients for the brine solution of three parts salt to one part baking soda. Add ice and water to chill the mixture. Soak the bait in the solution for five or six hours before bagging. This process will preserve the quality and appearance of the baitfish. The end result is a tougher, more natural-looking bait. To conserve the resource and maximize your efforts, store only enough bait in each bag for a single fishing trip.

Florida's master anglers have a lot to say about baitfish. The following discussion includes many of the more popular baits used by our master anglers in their specific area of Florida. Be aware there are many more baitfish types available to Florida anglers, and you need to keep your eyes and ears open for local alternatives.

Shrimp

In a sample of Florida master anglers, shrimp was the most popular natural bait identified. Shrimp can also be one of the easiest natural baits to acquire. A trip to a local bait shop will normally get plenty of shrimp for your day's fishing activity. However, live shrimp are not always available, and you may have to settle for freshly dead or frozen ones. Either live or frozen, they make great bait for almost all saltwater fish that Florida anglers target. Shrimp will normally guarantee success if you are fishing productive areas—and it doesn't matter if the shrimp are dead or alive.

As far as the sizes of the shrimp, it doesn't seem to matter to the fish. Very large redfish and snook will eat the smallest of shrimp if they have the opportunity. The problem is, with everything else in the water also wanting to eat shrimp, the opportunity may not arise; small shrimp are easy prey for the smaller fish such as pinfish and snappers. For that reason, many master anglers prefer to buy medium-size or larger shrimp, just because the small bait-stealing fish do not get them off the hook so easily. The opportunity for a larger fish is increased when the bait on the hook stays in the strike zone longer. Personally, I prefer fewer medium to large shrimp to more small ones, even though the fish themselves may not care. There are still anglers around that say, "For bigger fish, use bigger bait." However, when it comes to shrimp, if you put a small shrimp in front of a big fish, you are likely to hook up.

There are many different ways to pin a shrimp on a hook. As a personal choice, I normally use Daiichi Bleeding Bait circle hooks. Once an angler becomes accustomed to *not* setting the hook, as they would with conventional hooks, the circle hook is a very effective tool. It also adds an element of conservation to fishing. Circle hooks almost always hook a fish in the corner of its mouth, thereby increasing the chances that a released fish will live.

Capt. Jim Savaglio fishes the West Coast in the Tampa and Sarasota area. He targets redfish in the mangroves with live medium-to-large shrimp. "I prefer to hook the shrimp in the horn area, across the body, and just in front of the dark spot. That hooking method allows the shrimp to swim or crawl naturally." Captain Savaglio uses a float and split-shot to drift the rig under the vegetation or up against the mangrove roots. When he uses a float he adds a leader that accommodates the depth of the water. On other occasions he simply omits the float and freelines the shrimp to his fishing location. In each application, he uses circle hooks. "I've used circle hooks with great success in recent years, usually a size one or one-ought. I always utilize a snell knot to tie the leader material to the hook."

Captain Savaglio says many anglers tend to reel too fast when setting the circle hooks, pulling the bait away from the fish. To mitigate this tendency he explains that a reel with a 6:1 ratio will retrieve about six inches of line for every turn of the handle. Turning the handle five or six times will pull the bait back three feet toward the boat and away from the fish. Hooking up a red or other fish using this technique amounts to this: "Bobber under, reel gently to take up the slack." The circle hook takes care of the rest.

For maximum action, I tie the circle hook to the leader with a loop knot, which gives the live shrimp a little more wiggle room. Even with dead shrimp, the loop knot will work fine without any major disadvantage. I normally pinch the fantail off and insert the point of the hook into the exposed flesh, and then string it on like you would a worm. Depending on the size of your hook, bring the point out of the back of the shrimp to finish the job. Pinching off the fantail also allows more scent to be released from the shrimp, sometimes stirring up a feeding frenzy.

If the shrimp is dead, you can do just the opposite. Pinch off the head and throw it overboard as chum. Dead or frozen shrimp often become very unstable where the head connects to the body. If you hook them in the head, as some do a live shrimp, the tail often separates from the head and you lose it on the cast. To prevent this separation, insert the point of the hook into the exposed flesh where the head was removed and bring it out the belly of the shrimp. But either way, dead or alive, shrimp makes excellent bait.

Dead or alive, rigged on circle hooks or jig heads, shrimp are a preferred bait by many master anglers.

For Capt. Richard Grathwohl a live shrimp is his first choice for bonefish, permit, and tarpon on the flats of the Florida Keys. Captain Grathwohl guides out of Marathon and likes live shrimp. He says, "They work the best in all conditions. That includes days with no wind, as well as windy days." He also reminds us that getting live shrimp is simply a matter of going to the tackle store or bait shop and making the purchase. Given the low profit-margin markup on shrimp, he advises anglers to buy some of their other tackle at the shop as well. If all we buy from the small local tackle shops is bait, they will soon be out of business. Your support of the store by purchasing other products will help them succeed and continue to provide a source of live shrimp.

Captain Grathwohl also gives some great pointers for using shrimp. "On bonefish, it is best to cast out in front of the fish and let the bait lie until the bonefish finds it." On permit, he suggests casting out in front of the permit and then reeling relatively fast, while holding the rod high. This method will skip the shrimp on the surface. When the permit charges the bait, stop and let the shrimp fall. "The permit will chase the falling bait to the bottom, and all you have to do to set the hook is lift up on the rod."

For tarpon, Captain Grathwohl casts out in front of the fish and reels in slowly. "The tarpon will follow the shrimp, open up, and inhale the bait." To set the hook, he recommends striking with several short deliberate jabs for best success.

Mullet

Mullet are one of the so-called baitfish that people also like to eat. Restaurant menus will have mullet listed as fried, grilled, or smoked, and it is a favorite of many anglers and non-anglers alike. Mullet are a hearty baitfish, but not always available. They are vegetarians so they don't normally bite on hook and line. Mullet are caught with a cast net. There are different types of mullet in Florida, but most people refer to finger mullet or silver mullet when talking about mullet as bait. The finger-mullet designation is given because of

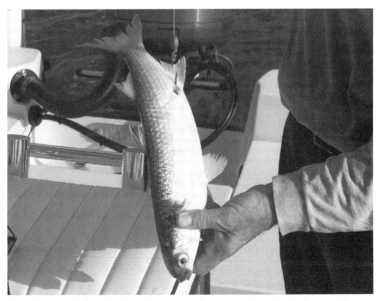

Pinned on a 7/0 live-bait hook, large mullet are an Everglades favorite for catching big snook.

their size, about the size of a finger. They make great baits, dead or alive, for almost any fish you target.

The striped mullet is a larger variety that is used whole for targeting really big fish or cut up and used in chunks when smaller baits are needed. When I think of big mullet, I always think of my good friend Capt. Pat Kelly and fishing in the Everglades.

Captain Pat is president of the Florida Guides Association and an expert snook fisherman. One October morning, we left out of Everglades City in search of big mullet to use for big snook. They were not particularly easy to find that day, but the first couple of throws of the cast net produced some 10- to 12-inch mullet. Captain Pat proclaimed that "they would have to do." Believe it or not, he was complaining because they were so small. I couldn't believe I would be using such a large mullet for bait.

We continued on with our "little" baits to one of Captain Pat's snook holes. He carefully pinned a Mustad 7/0 bait hook through the belly of the beastly mullet, near the anal fin. He explained that he wanted the hook to come out of the bait easily when the snook strikes. The angler has to heave the big bait out on a rod with plenty of backbone. Captain Pat instructed me to wait for the *thump* and then set the hook hard. It all went as planned. After a short wait, I felt a distinct thump on the line, I set the hook hard, and a giant snook came flying out of the water. Maybe there is something to that saying, "If you want big fish, use big bait."

Well, that was the Everglades and the big mullet worked fine. However, on the East Coast flats, where I fish most often, finger mullet are the bait of choice for many master anglers. An easy and effective way to hook the mullet is through the upper lip. Begin the hook inside the mouth and come out of the top. This part of the mullet is tough and can withstand numerous casts without the hook pulling free. Hooked in this manner, the mullet tend to live well and can be freelined around the perimeter of a school of mullet for reds, snook, and sea trout. Mullet can be hooked the same way on a slip-sinker rig for flounder and other bottom-feeding fish.

To set your mullet to swim under docks, mangroves, or other structures, a hook placement through the back behind the dorsal fin

This "mogan" snook was caught on a huge mullet in a river that flows through Everglades National Park.

is a good choice. This placement tends to cause the mullet to swim away from you and back under the structure. Leave the bail open and feed line to allow the least resistance. A hungry snook or redfish just can't resist the sight of this lively bait swimming right into its shady lair.

Finally, don't forget Captain Van Horn's backup bait. Cut dead mullet can be a day-saver when live ones are not available, and sometimes the cut mullet yields better results. Always use circle hooks with dead bait to ensure a clean hookup in the corner of the fish's mouth and an easy release of the fish.

Pinfish

The pinfish is a favorite of many master anglers. This hardy fish can be used on a variety of fish with good success. Pinfish are found throughout Florida, inhabiting the grass flats and estuaries as well as around sunken debris.

Clipping the dorsal and tail fins from a pinfish will make it easier prey for lazy fish. Photo by Capt. Chris Myers.

This durable baitfish can be caught in a variety of ways. Capt. Chris Myers says, "A small piece of shrimp or squid on a tiny hook cast into a shallow sand hole will usually bring quick results. You can also bait up a sabiki rig with tiny bits of shrimp and catch multiple baits with each cast."

Pinfish can also be caught in cast nets, thrown over these same sandy pot holes. Chumming in an area with bits of shrimp will also increase your catch. Commercial pinfish traps are also available and can get you a day's supply of baits while you sleep.

Captain Myers likes to rig pinfish on circle hooks, pinned through the nose and sight-cast to schools of redfish. He says, "Clipping the dorsal and tail fins will make your bait easier for lazy fish to catch. They can also be rigged under a float and fished while at anchor for both redfish and trout." If fished without a float, they tend to seek out cover in the grass and will not be nearly as effective.

Capt. John "GiddyUp" Bunch prefers pinfish over any other natural bait. He says there are other good baits, such as the Spanish sardine or the Atlantic threadfin herring, but "No bait is as hardy and resilient as the pinfish. Under a cork float for tarpon, tripletail, and redfish, 'pins' are deadly baits." Captain GiddyUp is among those master guides who like to clip the tail to slow down the bait, in case the targeted predator is a little lazy and doesn't want to work too hard for a meal.

Captain GiddyUp carries several cast nets on his boat for use in different water depths. Deeper water requires a larger net that will sink fast before the bait can run out from under it. He also has a secret that allows him to catch his bait. "I deploy a HydroGlow fish light before dawn, and just before I throw the net, all lights are turned off. Just as people can't see well when the lights go off suddenly, the fish can't either." This little trick of using a fish light reduces the number of times you have to throw the net to get enough bait.

Pinfish also work well as cut bait. Cut them in steaks leaving the skin on both sides and pin them to a 4/0 or 5/0 circle hook and an appropriate weight for your fishing conditions. You can freeze pinfish for later use, but most master anglers prefer to use fresh-cut pinfish.

Pigfish

The pigfish, a member of the grunt family, is sometimes mistakenly identified as a pinfish because of the similarity in their size and shape. They can be obtained in the same manner described above for pinfish. Cast-netting over chum, small hook-and-line fishing, or using the commercial pinfish traps will work just fine. Pigfish are relatively hardy, and make choice bait for big spotted sea trout and other saltwater predators.

When pinned on a circle hook and freelined over grass flats, their natural tendency is to swim down into the grass to hide. A lift of the rod and a couple of cranks on the reel will raise them out of the grass and also cause them to produce a grunting sound. That grunt is often their downfall. Predator fish will come from great distances to check out the sound and then devour the pigfish.

The repeated lifting out of the grass to reveal the bait and create the grunt takes its toll on the pigfish. Keep a good eye on the action and liveliness, and replace it when its action slows. They simply are not as effective when they loose their liveliness and the ability to create the grunting sound. Master anglers say that grunting sound is equivalent to ringing the dinner bell for hungry fish.

Ladyfish

Ladyfish not only make great bait dead or alive, they also are fun to catch. Often referred to as poor-man's tarpon, ladyfish exhibit a tendency to fly out of the water when hooked. More times than not, this aerial display of the ladyfish results in throwing the hook and a quick escape to freedom. Easily caught on hook, bait, or artificial lures, the sometimes lowly regarded ladyfish is excellent bait for many saltwater fish and excellent entertainment for anglers.

Captain Van Horn says, "I like to let my clients catch them on either jigs or top-water plugs. This gives my clients a chance to warm up, and it gives me a chance to evaluate their fishing skills."

Ladyfish tend to run in schools, and once found, are easily targeted for harvest. They can be used live or cut into chunks or strips for use as dead bait. Cutting a fresh ladyfish provides a smell that attracts the predators and a tasty flesh to make them hold on once they bite. Even the head can be used as bait, but many master anglers throw out the head and tail as chum and use the freshly cut steaks or strips as bait. As with most cut baits, circle hooks are the preferred method of fishing chunked or stripped ladyfish.

Captain Van Horn identifies fresh-cut ladyfish as his number-one dead bait. "When I cut ladyfish up, I cut large steaks and place the chunks in a plastic container. Store them on ice, and they will have better flavor and retain their firmness." One of the drawbacks of the cut ladyfish is that catfish like it too. Captain Van Horn suggests using larger chunks for this very reason, as larger chunks wider than three inches are difficult for the catfish to swallow.

Capt. Ed "Jazz" Jazwierski likes using ladyfish in chunks when fishing mangrove roots on high water. He says, "Put a chunk on a circle hook with a little weight, and throw it under the bushes. If there are redfish around, they'll sniff out that chunk of bait for sure. It's a great way to bring the fish nearer to you and out from underneath the mangrove roots that might be impossible to fish other-wise."

The Florida record for ladyfish is more than 4½ pounds, so don't think of them only as baitfish. They make a great recreational catch as well. Where you find one, there are usually others around—and the big ones will even pull a little drag.

Scaled Sardines

Scaled sardines, often referred to as whitebait, are excellent bait. These lively baits can either be cast-netted or caught on a sabiki rig. In either case, a little chum will help attract them to your net or hook. Except for the cost of a cast net and chum, scaled sardines are free. The cast net will pay for itself when you switch from buying dozens of shrimp to netting sardines.

Captain Jazz likes to use scaled sardines for a number of reasons. He says a cast net, a can of jack mackerel (for chum), a can opener, and a little time will usually produce the bait you need for a day's fishing. The only real variable is the time; "Sometimes two minutes and sometimes two hours," he says. He cautions anglers to take good care of the sardines once obtained. "When the bait is in the livewell, run the pump constantly to keep the water fresh and aerated. Don't overcrowd your livewell with bait or they will die."

Scaled sardines are very versatile and can be used for many fish species. Captain Jazz says, "Just about everything from an eight-inch redfish to a hundred-pound tarpon will eat scaled sardines. They are very hardy in the livewell and on the hook."

Another frequent user of scaled sardines is West Coast guide Capt. Robert McCue. He says the sardines are basically the filet mignon of piscivorous Florida fish. "They are hardy saltwater shin-ers and a natural food source for predatory game fish. They are a critical and vital source of protein, energy storing, fat building, and oil saturation for reproduction and egg development during the warmer months."

Unfortunately, this popular baitfish is not available all year. The life cycle of the scaled sardine includes migration, spawning, and

For game fish in Florida, scaled sardines are like candy to a baby. Photo by Capt. Robert McCue.

hatchlings. When the cycle ends in fall, the fish become less available. Even when they can be found, the game fish may not react to them as well. Captain Rob says, "As they cycle out, offshore or southward, shrimp begin to migrate inshore and then the fish seem to key in more on the shrimp."

Given their popularity with fishing guides and other anglers, scaled sardines are a fishery themselves. Captain McCue says, "Where to get them, how to catch them, and where to get the right sizes are skills top guides develop over decades if not lifetimes." He uses custom-made, ten- and twelve-foot cast nets to catch them. During periods of warmer temperatures, they are most often chummed over the grass flats inside the passes. Captain McCue's chum is a mix of bread, canned sardines, and menhaden oil. Some guides add other ingredients, such as anise oil, oatmeal, and cornmeal. Sand can be added to get the chum to dissipate in different depths or areas of stronger currents.

When the bait is around in cooler temperatures, they don't chum as well, and other techniques are needed. Under cool conditions, Captain McCue will drift and look for bait schooled on the bottom and throw a cast net on them. Alternatively, he will use what's known as rodeo-driving to get his day's supply. He describes rodeo-driving as a method to get bait when chumming doesn't work. The basic way is to idle along until you see the bait, shut down, load your net, drift until you see it again, and then throw. Another way is to idle along with the net loaded as you stand behind the console. When you see the bait, disengage the engine, run to the bow, and throw.

Rodeo-driving can also be accomplished by a team effort. Guides in particular use this method when they are already in the same area and chumming is not working. One guide will anchor his boat and board the other boat. As one guide drives the boat the other loads the net for casting. The driver positions the boat so the netter can throw downwind and the search begins. When the sardines are spotted, the driver puts the boat into neutral, and the netter throws. If the outcome is as desired, the bait is put into the livewell. The bait is then split between the guides, and they continue with their respective charters.

According to Captain Rob, rodeo driving can be either very productive or a lot of work for nothing. It all depends on the tightness of the schools. Sometimes the bait stages over sand near the beaches away from the flats. They don't chum-up well in these locations, so rodeo is the technique to use. Captain McCue says, "They are usually massed tightly when not feeding, and catching them goes fairly quickly."

When the bait catching is slow, Captain McCue says he might have to settle for 100 baits instead of 600. However, he adds, at this point in the bait cycle, the fish will respond to just about any live baitfish, so he also keeps all the palm-size pinfish he nets as bycatch to have enough bait for the day.

As far as finding scaled sardines, anglers need to look for signs. If you see something that might indicate baitfish, go investigate. If you don't see the water surface appearing like sprinkling rain drops, the bait may be deeper, and you'll need to recognize other signs. Captain McCue says, "A single tern swooping could be revealing the bait. Birds such as pelicans also reveal bait locations when they high dive with a half corkscrew entry to get deeper. They are responding to flashing bait that they see deeper in the water column." Once a spot is revealed and confirmed to be holding bait, Captain McCue marks the spot with his GPS.

Menhaden

Menhaden, or pogies as they are also called, are one of my favorite baits for the nearshore Atlantic Ocean. Like many of the other bait-fish, they can at times be difficult to catch, while other times it seems almost effortless. Pogies are filter feeders. Without getting into too much science, pogies eat by straining suspended food particles from the water. They actually play an important ecological role as they and other filter feeders remove suspended matter from the water, leaving it in a cleaner and clearer condition than before. Because of their feeding habits they are not targeted by hook and line but by anglers throwing cast nets.

Menhaden are a very oily fish and leave an oily slick when trolled. They also have a distinctive odor that adds to their fish-attracting properties. They have long been sought after by commercial fisher-men for the production of oil and fish meal. Many anglers add com-mercial menhaden oil to their chum to give it an added attraction.

In order to cast-net menhaden, cruise an area while watching for diving birds or flicking action on the surface that suggests the

Diving and swarming birds are a good indication that baitfish are present and that predator fish won't be far away.

presence of baitfish. When the pogies are spotted flicking on the surface, move close and cast the net. They can move quickly and spook easily by an approaching boat so act quickly. Even when you see images on your sonar, it's no guarantee they will be there when you cast your net. It is best to see at least a couple of flicking baits before you throw or you might come up empty. Let the net sink to the bottom before pulling on the mainline to capture the bait inside. An eight- to ten-foot net works well, but in deeper water a twelve-foot net may be needed. If you carry only one net, a ⅜ mesh (one with holes ⅜-inch wide) would be the one. If you have the luxury of carrying additional nets, you might want one larger and one smaller than ⅜ inch, depending on the size of the bait you encounter. Put the pogies in the livewell without a lot of handling to insure their vigor. They are fairly hardy and will survive well if plenty of fresh water is continuously supplied.

When slow trolled in nearshore waters, menhaden will attract kingfish, tarpon, jack crevalle, bonito, sharks, and many other varieties. I like to use the single-hook stinger rig described in Chapter 3 and slow troll the live pogey for best results. If your idle speed is faster than about three knots, tilt your engine up to slow down the speed. This strategy also produces a very visible prop wash that gets the attention of curious predators. I have had kingfish and cobia strike a menhaden trolled as close as the far end of the prop wash.

If you choose to freeline the bait, you can either hook it through the nose or in the back above the anal fin. Either way will produce predators when fished around bait pods or above structure, or when cast to cruising tarpon, jacks, or cobia. When freelining the pogies, use a circle hook appropriate to the fish that you are targeting.

Menhaden also work well as cut bait and release even more smell than when used live. Cut the pogey in half, on the diagonal, from just behind the top of the head to just in front of the bottom of the tail. Pin the chunk on a circle hook through both sides of the open cut and cast them out. You can use them on a slip-sinker rig for bottom fishing or simply free lined with no weight at all. Leave them set, and let the smell permeate the area. If predators are around it won't take them long to find the bait.

Spanish Sardines

Spanish sardines can grow as long as nine inches and make a tasty meal for many saltwater fish. They are an oily fish that produces a scent trail that can be irresistible to predator fish. They are readily available frozen and often constitute the backup bait for those times when live finfish cannot be found. Once you thaw them, keep them on ice to preserve their quality because they tend to deteriorate quickly.

For live bait, Spanish sardines can be caught with cast nets, when the water is not too deep, or with sabiki rigs in deeper water. Use great care in unhooking the sardines from the sabiki rig and get them to the livewell without touching them. Make sure the livewell has good circulation, as these baitfish are not very hardy.

Spanish sardines can be fished near the surface by drifting the boat and freelining the sardines in an area where you expect the predators to be. Simply hook them through the nostrils and let them swim freely. You can either place the rod in a rod holder and wait for the screaming drag, or hold the rod and feel the bite for yourself. If there are any predators around, this bait is likely to get their attention.

Spanish sardines can also be used for trolling. Because of their oily nature, they create a slick that entices kingfish and other predators to eat. Capt. Keith Kalbfleisch is one of those captains who uses frozen Spanish sardines as his backup bait for trolling when live baits are not available. Captain Keith prepares a stinger rig that includes a flat jig head as the front hook. Add a piece of 40-pound stranded cable and a treble hook to complete the rig. Pin the sardine to the jig head by inserting the point straight up under the jaw and out the top of the head. Complete the rigging by placing one hook of the treble through the back leaving a little slack in the wire cable. Captain Kalbfleisch dresses the whole thing up by adding a Mylar king buster or similar accessory for color. The Mylar skirts feed back over the jig head and the head of the baitfish. The flat surface of the jig head acts like a planer and prevents the dead sardine from spinning.

A flat jig head, stranded wire cable, a treble hook, and a Mylar accessory make a great trolling rig for frozen bait. The flat head on the jig keeps the bait from spinning.

This same rigging technique will work with other dead baits when you want to troll without the spinning motion often caused by dead baits. Vary the size of your flat jig head to accommodate the size of the bait. Large baits need larger jig heads to offset the spinning motion. Once the rig is set, Captain Keith advises setting your trolling speed a little faster than you would with live baits. He says, "I like to troll at about seven knots to keep the predators from getting too good a look at the bait and rig before striking."

Crabs

They can be caught by hook and line, using a big chunk of almost any dead fish or fresh chicken. Crabs can also be caught by baiting traps with dead fish and just waiting for the crabs to show up. Or, they can be bought live, whole, or frozen from area bait shops.

A fun way to catch them is by hand, wading along the shore at night, finding them with a flashlight, and dipping them with a dip net. Once a crab is spotted, simply keep the light on it while moving the dip net over and beyond the crab. Quickly sink the net into the bottom directly behind the crab and pull forward. If successful, you have great bait for your next fishing trip.

Silver-dollar crabs are a favorite natural bait for permit fishermen in the Florida Keys and other areas where permit roam. Capt. Dave Sutton, who guides out of the Keys, uses crabs for bonefish. "When using crabs I start the hook from the bottom side and drill it through one of the points on either side of the body. Work the barb through the shell very slowly and carefully to minimize the hole you make." An alternative method is to pull off a rear leg and use the resulting cavity as an entry point, then bring the hook out the top side of the shell. Being careful when you hook them will allow a crab to live as long as three hours on a 2/0 circle hook. He advises anglers to dangle the crabs in the water while you are poling and put them in the livewell while you are on plane.

Larger crabs, such as the blue crab, are used for tarpon, redfish, and black drum. They may be taken by hook and line after placing a chunk of dead fish on a line and letting the crab begin to eat. Chicken parts work equally well to tempt a hungry crab. Slowly bring the crab toward you until you can place a dip net under it to seal the deal. Be careful, they pinch and don't let go. It is a good idea to handle the crabs with either long-nose pliers or tongs. Many master anglers remove the claws to help avoid getting pinched. Removing the claws also adds scent to the water, which will help attract fish.

Blue crabs are also used successfully cut in half or quartered. Many master anglers first crush the crab to release more smell and then cut them in half or into quarters for bait. Keep the cut crab on ice and if you have any left over at the end of the day you can even freeze it for next time. Much like any cut bait, the crabs emit a strong scent and bring in predators from great distances to find an easy meal.

Cut crabs are often fished on a sliding-sinker rig that allows an easy pickup without a lot of drag on the fish. Leave the bail open and let the fish eat and swim away before reeling the circle hook into his jaw. Once tension is felt on the line and pressure is exerted on the rod, lift the rod firmly to ensure a good hook up.

Fiddler crabs are much smaller and used for sheepshead, pompano, and other shell cracking fish. Fiddler crabs inhabit rocky areas and can be found by moving the rocks and spotting them lying beneath the cover. Carry a small dip net and a bucket along with you to hold the crabs as you catch them. Put them on the hook with the same method as other crabs, by removing a leg and using the resulting hole as an insertion point for the hook.

Because fiddler crabs are found among the rocks, the fish that feed on fiddlers look for them around rocks. Using a float can decrease the number of times you hang up and break off in rocky areas. Use a 1/0 or smaller hook with a 20-pound leader. Add a small split shot for weight. When fishing for sheepshead around pilings or seawalls, scrape off a few barnacles for chum to attract the fish. When they see that fiddler crab hanging there it will look like an easy meal and you will be hooked up.

Bait-Catching Methods

For those anglers who catch their own bait, the main methods include cast nets, sabiki rigs, and fish traps. The choice of method depends on individual preference and local conditions.

Cast-Net Techniques

Most master anglers carry one or two and sometimes three different cast nets so they can successfully catch the baitfish they want. The size of the mesh and the weight of the lead determine the sink rate of the net. Size and weight of the nets is something you should determine for the area that you fish and the bait that you seek. Beginning netters should probably attend a seminar on throwing cast nets or, better yet, buy one of the videos available on the market. Calusa Cast Nets sells a great instructional video for about $20 that teaches the proper techniques of cast-netting.

Captain Jazz uses a Lee Fisher Bait Buster cast net. His choice is the model with a ten-foot radius with ⅜ mesh. He says this net sinks fast and catches the size of bait he wants, while allowing the smaller fry to escape through the mesh. It works well in two feet of water and well enough in deeper water when the need arises. At certain times of the year, when you're after bigger bait and want the smaller fish to be able to escape, he uses a net with ¼-inch mesh. Getting these smaller baits caught in a ⅜ mesh creates a big mess; if it happens you should clean them out immediately because they will begin to smell quickly in the Florida sunshine. The drawback of the smaller net is that you will have to cull out the smaller baits by hand.

Every once in a while, Captain Jazz likes to fill a five-gallon bucket half full of warm water and add some Downey liquid soap. Soak the net overnight, and rinse it thoroughly with fresh water. This process tends to keep the mono in the net from drying out. Hang the net up and let it dry before sealing it up in its bucket container. "If taken care of," he says, "a quality net will last for several seasons."

Captain Jazz also has a great piece of advice for throwing a net. He says, "As soon as you throw the net and it's still in the air, untether the line from your wrist and just hold on to it with your hand. If the net gets hung up on something you may need to let go quickly before being pulled overboard." Also, since you may get a lot of things in the net that you don't really want, it's wise to have a hand broom on board to sweep grass and other debris off the boat. "You will catch shells, starfish, seahorses, and other fishes. Make sure you return them to the water unharmed."

Another really great tip comes from Capt. Dave Sutton. "Patience with a cast net is one of the most important tips I can share. *Do not* throw the net multiple times on an iffy shot, because you will only make the quarry you are targeting spooky and more difficult to net." Captain Sutton suggests waiting for that perfect time to throw when the bait is visible and close together. "If you practice patience, you will usually get enough bait for the day on one throw instead of throwing ten times."

Some master anglers also place chum in an area to attract the baitfish. The chums range from homemade to commercially available products. Chum consists of finely ground fish parts. Some are of a wet variety while others are referred to as dry chum.

For West Coast guide Capt. Dale Fields, fresh chum is a necessity. His standard recipe includes a can of jack mackerel, a loaf of wheat bread, and a small bottle of anise extract for added flavor. Captain Dale says to try several mixtures to find what works best in your area.

Capt. Danny Guarino also guides on Florida's West Coast, where he likes to use scaled sardines. He uses a 10-foot ⅜-mesh cast net, but before he throws, he puts out some dry chum. The dry chum will begin to dissolve as soon as it hits the water driving the baitfish into a feeding frenzy, making them both plentiful and easy to net. Although he says there is no secret to it, he does add a little fish oil to sweeten up the mix. A variety of fish oils are available on the market, and you should experiment to find the ones that work best for you. The advantages of the dry mix include no need to refrigerate, less messy, and little waste. With the dry mix you can use just as much as you need without having to throw out the excess that you don't use.

Sabiki Rigs

Sabiki rigs are used to catch multiple baitfishes on one line. The normal sabiki rig contains six hooks and can be purchased in a variety of sizes depending on the bait you target. Daiichi is famous for their Bleeding Bait hooks and they make sabiki rigs with red hooks too. The rigs come with a swivel on the top side for easy connection to the mainline. Tied to the swivel is about four to five feet of 20-pound-test leader material. Attached to the leader are drop lines, about every eight to ten inches. The drop lines have what looks like a tiny fly secured to the end. The wings on the fly are normally made of fish skin. Finally, at the bottom end of the rig is a snap swivel which allows a proper-size weight to be easily fastened to the rig. The heavier the weight, the faster the sink rate.

Since small baitfish will hold around pilings, buoys, and other structures, these are likely areas to use a sabiki rig. Simply jig the sabiki rig vertically along side the structure until you find the depth where the bait is holding. Once you hook a couple of baits simply repeat the process at the same depth.

Potholes on shallow-water grass flats will also produce multiple hookups of lively baitfish on a sabiki. In this scenario you will use a smaller weight and pull the sabiki rig across the sandy potholes. You can use chum to get the feeding frenzy started then toss the sabiki in for quick results.

In deeper open water, a fish finder will come in handy. Sometimes baitfish will be suspended in open water and will only be located by a careful eye on your sonar. Once you find the bait and the depth, you should lower your sabiki below the ball of bait and then slowly jig your way up through it. It is not at all unusual to catch several baits at the same time.

When rigs right out of the package don't produce, you can bait the hooks with small pieces of shrimp, cut-up fish, or squid. Sometimes the added scent provided by the natural bait will improve your success. Most master anglers prefer using small pieces of squid to cut-up fish or shrimp because these stay on the hooks longer and eliminate the need to re-bait as often.

When targeting larger baits, some master anglers like to reduce the number of hooks to only three. This makes handling a multiple hookup easier and reduces the time you have the baitfish out of the water. Also have plenty of rigs on hand because it is not uncommon for a predator of the deep to nail one of your freshly hooked baitfish and be gone with your sabiki rig.

Always handle the baits carefully and place them in the livewell without touching them. If you can do this, their longevity will improve considerably. Some people simply shake them off the hooks, but a better method is to use a dehooker of some kind. There are special small versions on the market made especially for baitfish. I fished with one captain who used a simple butter knife from his wife's kitchen to remove bait from his sabiki. Simply place the blade against the shank of the hook and lift the knife while holding the drop line steady. As the hook inverts and the point is down the bait falls right off. Be sure you have positioned the bait over the well so it falls in the livewell and not on the deck, where you would have to handle it to get it in the well. Remember, the less you handle the bait the better.

These sabiki rigs were once a pain to deal with because of their potential to tangle, the likelihood of hooking something other than the bait, and the inconvenience associated with storing them. Angler creativity has successfully removed that burden. New bait poles on the market handily store the sabiki rig inside the hollow rod, with only the weight exposed on the end. They look somewhat like a conventional fishing rod, only greater in diameter. They are equipped with a seat to attach a reel. The angler simply threads the mainline from the reel through the center of the rod and attaches it to the swivel of the sabiki rig. When finished catching bait, everything except the weight is reeled inside the rod for safe, convenient storage. One final thing, the hooks on these rigs are very sharp. Be careful not to get them in you or in other soft materials such as a rope, tackle bag, or worse yet, another angler.

Bait Traps

If you want to catch your bait while you sleep, you can set out a trap the night before and pick up your bait the next day as you travel to your favorite fishing hole. Traps come in different sizes and types depending on what you want to catch. Simple in design, these baitfish traps are constructed with a cone-shaped entry hole for the bait to enter in search of a food source that you provide. Once inside the trap, the baitfish continue to feed on the easy meal you left for them. The shape of the entry holes make it difficult for them to escape.

Most traps have a place to put the food source so it does not dissipate rapidly. If you are leaving the trap overnight, you want to have a continuous supply of food to attract and hold the bait. Just follow the manufacturer's directions for securing the food in the trap. Mullet, ladyfish, or any fish carcass will work well. Cut fish will add more scent and create more of a feeding frenzy.

Placement of the trap is critical to your success. If, for example, you have previously caught pinfish on hook and line in an area, this would probably be a good place to set your trap. Find a sandy spot in a grassy flat and set the trap. The cut mullet or ladyfish you add to the trap will attract the baitfish. Give it at least a couple of hours to catch some bait or simply come back in the morning.

A tip from our master anglers suggests that once you lift a trap you should completely empty it into your livewell. If not, those trapped baits may escape upon return to the water because they are frightened and no longer interested in feeding, only in seeking freedom. If after a couple of hours no bait has been trapped, it will be necessary to move the trap to a new location.

Crabs can also be captured, but require a different type of trap. Recreational crab traps have sides that open up when the trap is lowered to the bottom. They provide a great way for anglers to catch crabs for bait. When the trap is raised the sides are pulled up, collecting the crabs inside. Dead fish can be used as bait and will definitely attract the crabs. Chicken necks are also great bait. The bone in the chicken neck can be secured tightly to the trap making it difficult for the crabs to remove it.

Last Cast

Consider this comment from Capt. Pat Dineen as food for thought. He says his preferred way to catch live bait is to trade a $20 bill for it. "Live bait takes time to catch, time you could spend fishing." However you get it, natural bait is on many anglers' wanted poster, and it is wanted, dead or alive!

Imitation of Life

Fishing with Artificial Bait

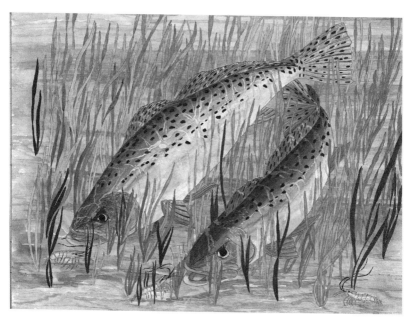

Nearly all anglers have heard the phrase, "Match the hatch." That's what artificial baits are all about, in the sense that they are an attempt to represent something that a game fish would find naturally when seeking food. Artificial baits are a model of the real thing. Capt. Blair Wiggins says when using artificial baits, "Be patient and keep trying. It's not like you see on TV all the time." He says, once you figure out how the fish want the bait worked, it actually gets a lot

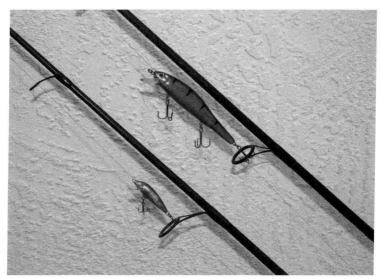

Artificial baits are all about matching the hatch. Most master anglers prefer smaller baits in the winter and larger ones in the summer.

easier. He suggests using artificial lures that imitate the bait type that is most predominate in the area at the time you are fishing. "If there are a ton of finger mullet around, throw something that looks like a finger mullet. Same goes with a scaled sardine. Throw baits that resemble a scaled sardine if that's all you see while fishing. If you get to your favorite spot and see no bait anywhere, but still suspect there's fish there, try an artificial shrimp. Shrimp are the most prolific bait that swims in salt water; that's why they're at the top of my list."

Today's artificial baits can be very realistic and detailed in design. Many of them have scales, eyes, fins, and every other feature of the real thing. The RipTide Mullet, for example, is very detailed in appearance. These lures have scales, fins, and a paddle tail that makes them swim like a real mullet. Rigging plastic baits on the RipTide Pro Jig Head adds realistic eyes to the presentation. Some lures may be designed to simply create a silhouette of a predator's intended prey, so when viewed at a distance, the lure draws a strike either out of hunger or sometimes out of anger. The old reliable spoon is a good example. It doesn't look to an angler like anything that swims in the water, but to the fish it produces a silhouette that could be a crab or even an injured mullet. Of course, it might also be looked at by the fish as an intruder and be struck at out of anger.

Fish encounter different kinds of natural baits during various seasons of the year, and this will influence the choice of artificial lures to use. The spring and fall mullet runs are excellent examples. During these times of the year, mullet imitations are good selections for the angler, although they will be good other times of the year as well. Winter on the flats sees fewer mullet, but more shrimp and crabs. Artificial crabs and plastic shrimp are a better choice in the winter.

In the previous chapter we found that artificial baits are often the backup of choice when natural bait cannot be found. In this chapter we learn that for many master anglers, fishing artificial lures is a preference. The preference is based on a simple challenge. Can I fool the fish into striking an artificial offering? Regardless of the reason, the angler is using the artificial bait in an attempt to convince some crafty old fish that the imitation of bait life is as good as the real thing.

Capt. Ray Markham, the well-known guide from the Tampa Bay area, sums up the position of those master anglers who prefer to use artificial baits exclusively as simply a personal preference. "I'd rather fool the fish than feed the fish," he says. "I use artificial baits, because for me, it's more productive and more of a pro-active approach to fishing versus sitting around waiting for a fish to come to my bait."

Because he uses artificial lures exclusively, Captain Markham never worries about those days when the bait just doesn't cooperate. In fact he says that's another good reason for using artificial as opposed to natural bait. In his mind he would rather be fishing than chasing bait.

Capt. Ron Tomlin feels the same way. "Fishing with artificial bait is true sportsmanship. Even if you don't catch as many as tossing a live bait, you have the satisfaction that comes with convincing a natural predator that they want to eat something totally out of their environment—you have to be good. It's pure sport, not high-production meat fishing."

Artificial lures come in all shapes and sizes. Pick the one that works the water depth you want to fish.

Today's artificial lures run the gamut from plastic to metal. They include wooden lures, hard-plastic lures, soft-plastic lures, metal lures, lead-head jigs, and whatever else the manufacturers and creative anglers can come up with.

Virtually any fish can be caught at one time or another on artificial lures, and some lures prove to be more effective than others. So, how do you find out which artificial lures have a history of producing fish? The best way to answer that question is to ask the experts what lures they find effective. By the way, remember the discussion about local knowledge? Artificial lures can have local applications as well. They may be effective in one area and not another, so be sure to ask at the local bait shops and marinas about artificial lures when you're checking with them on places to fish. They usually have the straight scoop and are happy to share it with you.

This chapter will reveal the "go to" baits of many of our master anglers and how to use them effectively. Let's begin with a discussion of one of the most popular and productive of the bunch: the soft-plastic lure.

Soft Plastics

Soft-plastic baits are a mainstay for many master anglers' tackle boxes. These soft plastics come in the form of baitfish such as mullet, shrimp, crabs, and almost everything else you find in the marine environment. Soft plastics are molded from a liquid plastic into their final bait-imitating forms. Some are impregnated with natural scents and other additives such as fish oil or fish parts. These additives appeal to a fish's sense of smell and taste and are aimed at making a fish strike and then hold on to the bait longer after biting.

Capt. Robert McCue likes to make fishing simple, and when he can't get his favored scaled sardines he chooses to fish with a jig. As a matter of fact, he says there is only one lure anyone ever needs anywhere in the world. He says it's a jig, because they work anywhere, anytime. He favors jigs because they are easy to use and cover a lot of water quickly. "When I am drift-fishing or trying to locate fish, jigs are my first choice. Now, with these new stink baits such as the Gulp, jigs function as very effective weight to hold them on the bottom for passing fish. Pinning a scented plastic lure on a jig head—commonly referred to as dead sticking—has become a highly effective technique among the redfish tourney guys."

Captain McCue thinks of lure colors as people colors. "People like how something looks, so they buy it. I am a firm believer in contrast and silhouettes. I use primarily two colors, a dark motor oil or root beer in dark water and under dark skies. I use chartreuse green in clear water and clear bright skies. I believe that fish, particularly at the times of year I use lures, are opportunistic feeders. If they can see their forage via contrast, or sense it through vibration in their lateral line, they will eat it. This is especially true during cooler weather when there is not much else around."

He does not like to crush the barbs on the jig-head hooks, unless he is fishing in areas of undersized trout, when trout are out of season, or after a limit of trout have been taken. He simply believes that all other species are resilient enough to withstand limited handling, but the trout are not. Trout need to be handled carefully and bending the barbs is a good practice if you are releasing them.

Even though he says you don't need anything but a jig, he does have other artificials in his arsenal. He refers to the other lures as his "special teams" and uses them in conjunction with the jigs. Topwater plugs for example can be helpful to locate fish with swirls, pops, or short bites. He then follows up with a jig to start catching those fish that were found using his special team on top. He also uses spoons and considers them a highly effective way to cover a lot of water, since they can be worked faster than a jig. Once a spoon attracts a fish such as a redfish, he suggests switching over to a jig and patterning the fish by using various speeds and retrieves until you find the one that is effective. Alternatively, once the fish are located, you can turn to the dead-sticking method to put the fish in the boat.

As far as advice to the angler, he says fishing is 90 percent confidence in what you are doing. "If you believe that a particular lure will work, you will fish it with confidence and catch fish with it."

There is no single best way to fish a plastic imitation and no single best lure, although most anglers have their own preference, which they refer to as their *go-to* lure. Different methods of presentation are required, depending on various factors such as water temperature, wind conditions, water clarity, and water depth. Captain Markham has his favorite. He says, "My favorite bait is the one that imitates what the fish are eating at the time—in other words, match the hatch." After selecting a bait to use, he then experiments with various presentations.

When guiding, Captain Markham likes to fish with his anglers, observing how the fish are responding to his presentation and compare it with his client's presentation and success. He then points out the difference and suggests a presentation for them to use. Obviously, you are looking for the one that works. "The one that works is the one I use at the time," says Captain Markham, "but just because it worked one day does not mean it will work the next." That means you often have to spend some time experimenting to find the pattern that's working on any particular day.

Finding a pattern is best described as a trial-and-error process. You might have to slow down your presentation, or you might have to speed it up. You might have to fish your lure deeper, or you might have to fish it higher in the water column. You might have to change colors, or you might have to add a rattle. Above all, you have to think about it. Don't continue to make the same unsuccessful presentation time after time. If you are not catching fish, try something different. If you still don't catch any fish, move the boat and try another spot.

Paddle-Tail Plastics

I use the RipTide mullet for prospecting and locating fish. This plastic bait has a paddle tail that produces a distinctive vibration and closely mimics a real swimming mullet. It can be rigged on jig heads of various sizes depending on the need. I normally use the three-inch version pinned on a RipTide Pro ¼-ounce jig head. This versatile lure can be used in many applications to accommodate wind, water depth, and water clarity. There are three colors I never want to be without. I always have electric chicken, nite glow, and silver mullet in my tackle box. Other colors work too, but over time, these three colors have been the most productive for me. Whatever the color, the idea is to produce a silhouette and movement that predators can quickly recognize as a possible meal, producing a hunger strike, or an unwanted invader of the fish's territory that might draw a strike out of anger.

The presentation of this lure is so simple a child can do it. Make a cast toward your intended target so it falls where you want it to land. You can stop the bait by closing the bail or by catching the line in the first knuckle of your index finger as Capt. Chris Myers described in Chapter 4. In deeper water you can let the lure fall before retrieving. In shallow water simply start your retrieve quickly, giving intermittent wrist flicks to change the action. Vary speeds and action until you get a strike.

Captain Markham also uses a paddle-tail lure as his top search bait. He uses the C.A.L. Shad from D.O.A. Lures to locate fish and find patterns. He says he works it quickly most of the time. He feels that a fast presentation creates a scenario that causes a reaction strike from fish that may not be hungry but will strike at something invading its turf. He recommends twitching the rod to make the bait swim erratically as a confused or frightened baitfish would do. As far as how to do it, he describes it as "start, stop, reel, and twitch, all at varying paces."

He goes on to explain that newcomers to using artificial baits should find a large swimming pool or some body of water that's clear enough to see the bait's action under different conditions. Pay particular attention to how the bait swims when you twitch the rod, speed up or slow down the retrieve, or just crank the bait back to you. Once you've used the bait successfully in various conditions, such as cold weather, hot weather, windy days, overcast skies, murky or stained water, or any other fishing condition, then do the same thing when you encounter those conditions again. It's all about finding a successful pattern.

Remember the question, "How do you get to Carnegie Hall?" Developing patterns is one more example of the importance of practice. Finding fishing patterns is part of the learning process needed to become a master angler. Captain Ray continues, "Knowing how fast the bait is swimming and what action it has will make the new user of artificials aware of what action fish are most attracted to, under different scenarios." It should be noted that this notion of patterning applies to the use of all artificials, not just plastics.

Plastic Jerk Baits

Although he uses paddle-tail baits as well, Captain Myers prefers plastic jerk baits when sight-fishing the flats. "If I could pick only one lure to fish the flats all year round, it would be the four-inch D.O.A. C.A.L. jerk bait, in gold or Arkansas glow. This lure is my choice because it will catch fish every day under different conditions, and it can be fished weedless."

Captain Myers likes the four-inch C.A.L. in the winter, because the redfish are targeting small baits naturally and the C.A.L. jerk bait matches the hatch. Even in the summer, when reds tend to be a little finicky about what they eat, he still uses the same bait to trigger strikes. He likes the color gold, but he keeps some handy in shades of green, such as olive, baby bass, or melon, as a backup if the gold isn't working. Captain Myers adds this advice about using plastic jerk baits. "In most situations people who are not catching fish on artificials are working the lure much too fast. You will rarely work most artificials too slow, but you can definitely go too fast. Presentation is much more important than color."

Captain Myers says many anglers have little confidence in artificial baits and will switch too quickly to natural bait if they are not getting constant action. His suggestion for those anglers is to take the time to practice if they want to improve their success rate. "I suggest to people that they go fishing without any natural bait on the boat. This will force them to spend time learning to use artificial baits. Personally, I will throw a lure I think will work until I have

Plastic jerkbaits can be rigged in many different ways. All are highly productive.

three fish in a row refuse it. Then, I will change lures, generally to something smaller."

Capt. Rick Burns is also a believer in plastic jerk baits. His go-to bait is the RipTide Flats Chub in white, pearl, electric chicken, or gold 'n glow. Captain Burns fishes the shallow water of the Gulf of Mexico outside Homosassa. He rigs weedless and fishes over grass beds, rock piles, and oyster beds in one to five feet of water. "Unlike natural bait," he says, "the angler has to make the jerk bait do what it is designed to do. That is usually an erratic, fluttering, jerky, injured-bait type of movement. Anglers can accomplish this action by giving short, slow jerks with the rod to make the artificial act and appear like an injured or disoriented baitfish."

Plastic Shrimp

A plastic bait found in most master anglers' tackle box is the plastic shrimp. Many versions of this versatile bait look exactly like the real thing and some are even scented to smell like the real thing. Since almost every fish in the water likes to eat shrimp, you never know what you might catch on this imitation of life.

Remember before, when Captain Myers said you can never fish plastic bait too slow? Slow is definitely the operative word when fishing with plastic shrimp. Capt. Ed "Jazz" Jazwierski agrees, "If you are fishing a plastic shrimp, fish it slow. Slow is what a shrimp does naturally. Cast it out, let it sink until it touches bottom, raise the rod tip, let it sink slowly again back to the bottom." The strike in this scenario will often come as the shrimp settles back toward the bottom. Using braided line gives the angler an excellent "feel" for the bite and also improves the hook-up rate, since braids do not stretch. The bite can be so subtle the sensitivity of the braided line is a great advantage to have when the bite occurs.

Captain Markham particularly likes a plastic shrimp in the winter when the fish become lethargic and are not aggressive feeders. Just as described before, he uses a C.A.L. shad bumped along the bottom to find the fish and once he finds them he turns to the plastic shrimp. He says, "Everything I fish for eats a shrimp, and this bait is the best of its kind." He prefers the D.O.A. shrimp with a Woodies rattle inserted. The rattle adds one more dimension that will attract fish to the bait. Markham says the D.O.A. shrimp can be skipped or cast to fish without spooking them, and the single hook makes for easy release. "The attitude of the bait with the hook riding up always provides the most natural-looking appearance, and it is also nearly weedless."

Captain Wiggins likes plastic shrimp too. "If I could choose one and only one artificial bait it would have to be a three-inch gold glitter D.O.A. shrimp, and I would use it anywhere. All the fish we love to catch eat shrimp. Just work it like a real shrimp swims, slow, slow, slow." Captain Blair prefers gold glitter, especially for reds and trout, but adds that glow and holographic are excellent for snook and tarpon. Captain Blair does not normally bend back the barb, because with experience, he says an angler can set the hook before the fish gets the lure too deep. However, if he finds the fish to be overly aggressive, he will remove the J-hook and replace it with a circle hook, which almost guarantees a hookup in the corner of the mouth.

As far as advice on presentation, Captain Blair says, "Work any bait in the manner of what it's imitating. When you finally get a hit remember how you were working it and repeat the action. This is easier said than done, since you tend to get an adrenaline rush when a fish strikes artificial bait."

Capt. Troy Mell's favorite plastic bait is actually one he helped develop. Captain Troy and his tournament fishing partner, Capt. Jason Swensson, researched it, tested it, and patented it. The bait is called the Yum Houdini Crab and is a combination crab-shrimp creation. Captain Troy says, "Because it is the only soft plastic that can be two different baits, it gives me flexibility without wasting time. The Yum Houdini Crab can be fished as a crab, drifting on the surface for tarpon or with a light jig head for sight-casting to redfish, snook, trout, and permit."

When fished whole, the lure imitates a crab, and the shrimp tail balances the whole lure for a no-twist retrieve. A quick tear-away portion of the lure converts the crab body to a shrimp with a smaller profile that will fall in the water column faster. The list of saltwater fish that feed on shrimp and crabs gives an angler plenty of opportunities for a hookup. Captain Troy's favorite colors are smoke, gold flake, white, glow, and root beer.

Like so many other master anglers he advises, "Be patient and match the lure to the bait in the area you are fishing. Also, vary the speed of your retrieve until you find the one that brings on the strike." Ending on a note of conservation, Captain Mell reminds anglers to "Make sure you dispose of any plastic bait properly. Keep the used ones until you get home and throw them out in the trash, not in the water."

Captain Jazz re-emphasizes the concept of fishing any plastic bait slowly. "Just when you think you are fishing it slow, slow it down some more. Trust me on this, you'll catch more fish."

Bucktail Jigs

A close cousin and actually a forerunner to most of today's plastic baits is the bucktail jig. Unlike the plastic baits described above, the body of this bait cannot be removed and replaced. The name bucktail comes from the fact that the original lures were made by tying hair from the tail of a deer to a jig head. The natural hairs of the deer were thought to be a natural attractant to fish. Today, natural or synthetic fibers are tied or glued to the jig head. Some anglers consider this a great advantage, because the fibers do not come off as do plastic tails, leaving the angler more time with bait in the water, instead of tying on a new rig.

Capt. John "GiddyUp" Bunch is a strong proponent of the bucktail jig. He says, "My favorite artificial is the white bucktail. Nothing else comes close." Captain GiddyUp says the white bucktail can be used for any fish. "What looks more like 'white bait' than a white bucktail?" He bends down the barbs out of simple sportsmanship, in an effort to give his adversary every chance for survival. As far as working the bucktail, he gives this advice, "Slow down and get in tune with your surroundings and treasure every moment as if it were your last. It just might be." He goes on to describe his presentation as one of seducing the fish. "Few anglers understand how to seduce a fish. It is via the rod tip and the wrists control the rod tip. A person versed in the art of fish seduction understands that the first kiss is with the wrist and this has nothing to do with turning a reel handle." So, fish a bucktail slow and allow the undulating fibers to seduce the fish into striking what appears to be a baitfish in distress, moving along very slowly in relation to other bait.

Slow is not the only way to present a bucktail jig. Some anglers like to add a long plastic eel to a bucktail when targeting free swimming cobia. In this adventurous form of sight-fishing, anglers travel the nearshore waters looking for a cruising cobia. Once sighted, make a cast out in front of the fish, so it will see the bait and follow it as it sinks toward the bottom. Eels are a mainstay in the cobia diet and this presentation, of a plastic eel on a bucktail jig, has proven to be too good to refuse by many a hungry cobia.

Topwater Baits

It may be a skyrocketing kingfish nearshore Canaveral or a West Coast redfish knocking a Top Dog to the sky, but most anglers agree, to have a big fish blow up on a topwater lure is one of the biggest adrenaline rushes available when fishing. The visual aspect of seeing the fish come out of the water, in an attempt to eat a floating plug, is at the top of the scale for fishing excitement. Anytime the fish are feeding on top, it brings the angling experience to a whole new level. So, which bait do you choose to create that level of excitement? Our master anglers have their favorites, as well as tips on how to use them.

Captain Jazz says he will take any topwater or gurgling-type artificial when it comes to just plain fun fishing. "You'll get fewer strikes on top, but they often make up for it in size. Some of my largest sea trout have been on topwater plugs, in water less than two feet deep." Captain Jazz also says topwater baits can be used as search baits, by fan casting them on the flats or working them down a mangrove stand. "If you get a follow or a half-hearted strike, cast again, if nothing happens, switch to something subsurface. You know fish are around, even if you only saw one or two." As a rule of thumb, Captain Jazz likes the water temperature to be 70 degrees or greater for best success with topwater presentations.

Capt. Ron Tomlin also uses topwater lures as search baits. He says he likes to use his favorite, a MirrOlure Top Dog Jr., anytime he is fishing the Everglades backcountry. "I use it to help locate fish because I can cover a lot of area. I find that it attracts not only feeding strikes, but also reaction strikes. I fish topwater until I locate fish. If they don't continue to take it, I'll throw a shallow diver like a Catch 5 or Catch 2000." His personal favorite colors are chartreuse, black with a white belly, green with a white belly, and the old reliable red head with a white body.

He says the main thing to remember, when using any artificial, is that you are trying to get a natural predator to look at your bait as something it would normally eat or something it doesn't want around. He says, "You have to move your bait in a manner that ei-

Early morning and a topwater lure make the perfect combination for fish in the mangroves.

ther attracts or enrages the predator you are after. Try different retrieves until you find one that works and do not be afraid to try any speed, or any action."

Captain Tomlin bends back the barbs on all his plugs to protect the fish and make it easier to remove the hooks. "I am primarily a catch-and-release guide, so assuring safe fish removal is essential to me." Needless to say, bending back the barbs, especially on treble hooks, is also a good idea to prevent the angler from taking a trip to the hospital if a mishap occurs.

Although not a given, most master anglers like to work a topwater plug in a zigzag motion. This erratic movement is referred to as "walking the dog." It can be accomplished in different ways, but the most common way is to hold the rod tip high and make quick deliberate snaps of the wrist to give the back and forth movement. It is actually the slack produced in the line, by the wrist movement, that allows the head of the bait to move one way, before being pulled back the other, producing the zigzag. Some master anglers produce this same action by using the crank on the reel to vary the speed and produce the slack. Regardless of how you do it, that zigzag action just seems to be something fish cannot resist.

Other topwater baits include chuggers and prop baits. They are effective because of the great commotion they cause on the water's surface. Think about it: These baits are essentially creating what looks like a feeding frenzy, as they splash and chug across the water. The chuggers push water ahead of them. The prop baits create a prop wash that follows the lure. Both types are generally fished in an erratic pattern of jerking, resting, jerking twice, resting, etc. Vary the pattern to create a situation where fish will either strike out of hunger (they don't want to miss out on the feeding frenzy), or they simply strike out of anger in reaction to all the commotion.

When using prop baits, I like to use a slashing retrieve that moves the bait quickly forward, let it rest, then slash again. I personally hold the rod low to keep the bait from coming up and out of the water. I also vary the slashing action. The pattern could be slash, rest, slash, slash, rest, etc. It is the same as with all artificial baitfishing, try different actions until you find the pattern that works. Then stick with the pattern until it is no longer producing fish.

Crankbaits

Crankbaits, as the name implies, are artificial baits that actually get their action from cranking the reel at various speeds on the retrieve. Throw them out and simply crank them back. Over the years, lure manufacturers have gone to great length to create lures that swim like the real thing when cranked. These lures vibrate, rattle, and dive—all depending on how fast the angler cranks the reel handle. Some of the more popular ones are lipped plugs such as Bombers, Rapalas, and Rebels. The size and shape of the lips on these plugs actually determines how deep they will dive and how much they will wiggle.

Captain Wiggins says he likes crankbaits that look like a pinfish when he's chasing redfish around rock piles or around jetties. His favorite is the silver Rat-L-Trap, because it looks like a pinfish or a sardine. As far as presentation goes, just crank the bait without ever

A creative crankbait, produced by LaserLure, has a red laser light built into the body. The light is activated when the bait hits the water. Different shapes give different action.

stopping. "I may slow it down, but I'll rarely stop it from moving." Remember, the action of the crankbait is produced by its retrieve, so you just keep them moving, trying different speeds until you find the one that produces fish.

Captain Markham says he doesn't use crankbaits much, but agrees they are a relatively easy bait to use. When he picks one up, he likes either a Bomber Long A, Rapala Original, or the Bite-A-Bait Fighter. His favorite colors are the same ones he likes for plastics, either gold-black back, silver-black back, or chartreuse-green back. Captain Markham says, "Lipped baits can cover the upper portion of the water column or midrange, or even the top, depending on how you work it, so that makes it versatile. I mostly use them as no-brainer baits. You don't need much finesse to produce fish with them, and you can do very little wrong with them." He gives them to novice anglers to use, because of the lure's versatility and ease of use.

Captain Markham is a big believer in patterning fish and says the actual presentation of crankbaits will depend on how the fish are responding on any given day. He says, "The presentation can be a pop and let it float to the surface. It can be a steady pull down and let it float back up, or it can be a constant retrieve." If the fish don't hit any of those retrieves, he switches to reel, twitch, reel, pause, twitch, twitch—just a series of reeling, pausing, and twitching that is erratic will often produce a strike.

Patterning might also require changing lures. Thin-profile baits such as a Rat-L-Trap will give you a tight wiggle, where a fat-lipped plug will give a wider wiggle. A lipped plug with the line tie near the end of the lip will run shallower than one that attaches closer to the body. Even though they are relatively easy to use, they do exhibit different actions based on design.

Captain McCue is another master angler who doesn't use crankbaits often, but when he does he favors a Bill Lewis Rat-L-Trap. His main target is snook, but he has also caught many tarpon, jacks, and redfish on a Rat-L-Trap. Because he fishes them mostly at night in dark tannic water, he prefers dark purple or black for maximum contrast. He also likes to use them in winter, when "fishing deep for slow-moving, nearly lethargic fish." His main target is snook laid up in deep holes, river bends, and canals. "I fish them very slowly and just off the bottom with a steady retrieve. On occasion I will try to 'yo-yo' them slightly while bouncing off the bottom."

Capt. Bouncer Smith uses his share of crankbaits and has a unique tip for rigging them. He uses his method for fish that eat their food whole, such as snook, tarpon, trout, and grouper. He alters the hook system by first crushing the barbs on the treble hooks. He then uses a 3/0 or 5/0 Diiachi circle hook tied directly to the leader. Next, hook the circle hook through the eye on the plug where you usually secure the leader. Finally, add a small Owner rubber bead or a small piece of rubber band to the hook to prevent the lure from coming off. Captain Bouncer says, "Catch rates for tarpon more than triple with this method compared to using stock treble hooks on MirrOlures, Rat-L-Traps, or Rattling Raps." Bouncer takes all the trebles off when targeting tarpon and doesn't want to catch jacks or mackerel. He leaves the trebles on with the barbs crushed down when taking on all comers.

Crankbaits come in all shapes and sizes for a reason. The size of the body and shape of the lip determine how deep the lure dives and how much it wiggles. Thin bodies give a tight wiggle; longer lips give a deeper dive.

Remove the treble hooks from a crankbait and replace them with a 3/0 or 5/0 circle hook to increase the hook-up rate on tarpon and decrease the hook-up rate on jacks, mackerel, and other fish. Use a #3 soft bead or a piece of rubber band to secure the lure on the hook.

Other methods of altering or tuning crankbaits are used to increase productivity. Since depth is important to fishing, the ability to change the depth of the retrieve on crankbaits can mean the difference between catching and not catching. Changing the size of the lip will change the depth that the bait will dive. Longer lips dive deeper, shorter lips run shallower. This can be done in the field by starting with a long lip and snipping at it with cutting pliers until you get the depth you want. In reality, this is probably best achieved before you hit the water where more precision can be obtained. You can also change the depth by the position of your rod on the retrieve. If you want to run shallow hold the rod higher. If you want to run deeper, hold the rod lower.

Once you start altering crankbaits, you have also altered the action built in by the manufacturer, so do it with caution. Your best bet is to test the lure in a swimming pool before fishing it for real. In the clear pool water you can observe what your alteration did to the plug and tune it even more. Watch the action on the plug and take out any unnatural movement. Bend the eye from side to side to make the lure run true and upright. Cast and observe again, until you get the movement you want. The goal is to adjust the crankbait so it doesn't pull to one side or lie over from the vertical plane.

Finally, some anglers like to swap out the hooks on the crankbaits. If the hooks are not already red, you can change them out to add the effect of wounded prey to the bait. I like to downsize the middle hook and upsize the back one. I have even drilled holes into my favorite crankbaits and inserted Woodies rattles to add the sense of sound. Just plug the drill hole with a little clear silicone after inserting the rattle. The ability to alter crankbaits to suit different conditions makes them flexible with the capacity to cover a lot of water when trying to locate fish.

Other Factors

There are a few other factors that affect the success of artificial baits. They include profile, color, and scent. Each of these different elements requires a specific decision on the part of the angler, in terms of which combination to use.

Profile

The shape and size of a lure can be an element of importance when fishing artificials. Yogi Berra is credited with saying, "You can observe a whole lot by just looking around." There is a whole lot of truth in his statement about observation and it applies directly to bait selection. Captain Markham says anglers should be observant of their surroundings. Monitor what kind of baitfish are in the area and ask questions such as, what kind of bottom are you fishing, what is the depth of the water, and where are the fish related to the depth? He says, "Choose lures that work the observed portion of the water column, and choose lures with a profile to match the bait you see." The shape and size of your lure determines the profile that the fish see, and the action you impart on the lure can actually change its profile. When retrieved through the water column, a paddle-tail jig imitates a swimming baitfish, but it appears to be a crustacean when bounced along the bottom. Captain Markham says the angler has to select the profile and provide the appropriate action. "While choosing bait with a certain profile, you can give it action that will appear to be another prey. How you work the bait can be as important as the actual bait at times."

Color Selection

Even though they each have their favorite colors, most master anglers agree: Color is not the most important factor in choosing artificial lures. The standard rule given by most master anglers says use darker colors for darker conditions and lighter colors for lighter conditions. Capt. Rick Grassett says, "I use light colors for clear water and bright sky and dark colors for overcast sky or cloudy water." His favorite light colors include silver, gold, chartreuse, and white. His favorite dark colors include root beer, green, or any kind of a dark-backed lure. He pays more attention to the color of the tail than the head but likes to contrast the two. "I like a light tail with a red head or a dark tail with a white or chartreuse head."

Agreeing that color is probably not the most important factor, Capt. Ray Markham has a certain attachment to nite glow and says the angler's confidence in a color is also important. "I think confidence in a color is just about as important as anything. I've found that nite glow produces fish in every scenario that I've fished, and it is my go-to choice of colors."

Scent

Smell, or olfaction, as scientists call it, is just one of the senses fish respond to. Fish have little holes that look like nostrils and take water in to be pumped into a chamber inside the fish. The chamber is filled with sensory pads that give fish the ability to smell as water is passed over the pads. With this knowledge, it makes sense to use a scented bait to improve your odds when fishing.

Some lures have scent built into them, while others require an outside source such as spraying or dipping. Common attractant products include Blast, a spray-on scent from Classic Fishing Products; Carolina Lunker Sauce, a dab-it-on product; Fish Bites, a synthetic product simulating natural bait; and a host of others, all aimed at creating a scent trail to bring more bites to your fishing. When the fish are not biting, it is always a good idea to do something different. Change colors, change profiles, or maybe just add some scent.

What's It All About?

Many master anglers describe fishing artificial baits as a challenge accompanied by a certain mental reward. Capt. Dave Sutton says, "Anyone can catch a fish using live or fresh natural baits, but using artificials is just that, a challenge." He reminds us that there are a whole lot of fly fishermen out there accepting the challenge, since every lure they use is artificial.

Captain Myers thinks anglers give up too quickly when using artificials. Instead, what they need to do is stick with it. Learning to use them correctly will pay big dividends in the future. A number of guides use artificial baits almost exclusively, and you can too. Captain Grassett is one who fits this category. "I use only artificial baits and flies—except for tarpon," he says. "I think it is most important to have confidence and to try different colors, retrieves, etc., until you find what works best for any given situation. Try to develop confidence in what you are using, and experiment with different techniques and speeds until you find what works best. This may vary from day to day, but your practice will pay off."

The word confidence keeps coming up when talking about artificial baits. An angler has to use them often to develop confidence, but once you do develop the belief that you can catch fish on your chosen artificial bait, you will have a go-to bait of your own.

Captain GiddyUp definitely has his favorites. He says, "My favorite three artificials are first, a Yo-Zuri Crystal Minnow in black and silver; second, the old standby gold spoon; and finally, a white bucktail jig." Captain GiddyUp says, "Life without live bait offers me the challenge to find out how good I really am. In my opinion having no live bait separates experts from amateurs."

Last Cast

There is a tournament in the Florida Keys that requires participants to select only one lure and fish the entire tournament with that one lure. This is the ultimate challenge in picking a lure in which you have complete confidence. Anglers are allowed to have replacements for lost lures, but they have to be the same size, color, and style.

The master anglers who are contributing to this book were informed of the rules of the one-lure tournament and asked the following question: "If you were going to fish and could choose only one lure, what would it be?" The results are reported in table 5.

The overall favorite was some type of jig with a plastic or bucktail body. It appears that the reason most captains chose a particular lure was because it would catch a variety of different fish. These types of lures can be controlled by the angler to fish different depths and create different profiles by changing the speed of the retrieve and the action imparted by the rod. These simple lures may look like shrimp, crabs, mullet, or almost any other natural bait that swims the seas.

Table 5. Master Anglers' Favorite Lures

Captain's Name	Favorite Lure	Favorite Color	What Will It Catch?
Bunch	Bucktail Jig	White	Anything, you name it
Burns	Johnson Silver Minnow	Gold Spoon	Redfish, Snook, Trout
Dineen	Bucktail Jig	White	Just about anything
Dunn	Johnson Silver Minnow	Gold or Silver	Redfish and more
Fields	Loves Lure	White	Most saltwater species, some fresh
Grassett	D.O.A. C.A.L. Shad Tail	Arkansas Glow	Red, Snook, Trout, Pompano, etc.
Grathwohl	Betts Halo Shrimp	Pink	Bonefish, Tarpon, Permit, & more
Guarino	Capt. Mike Spoon	Gold	Redfish, Snook, Trout
Jazwierski	Bucktail Jig	White	Anything that eats white bait
Kalbfleisch	Plastic Jerk Bait	White Belly,	Redfish, Trout, Tarpon, etc.
	D.O.A. or Bass Pro	Green or Black Back	
Markham	D.O.A. C.A.L. Shad Tail	Nite Glow	Snook, Trout, Redfish, & more
		Arkansas Glow	
McCue	Cotee Liv' Eye	Rootbeer or	Virtually all species
	Action Jigs	Chartreuse	
Mell	Yum Houdini Crab	Rootbeer	Redfish, Tarpon, Permit, & more
Myers	D.O.A. C.A.L. Jerk Bait	Arkansas Glow	Redfish, Trout, Snook, & more
Presley	RipTide Mullet	Nite Glow	Reds, Trout, Snook, & more
Savaglio	Gulp Jerk Shad	Pearl White	Reds
Smith	Spro Bucktail	White/Green and	All varieties
		Black Trim	
Sutton	Rapala X-Rap #10	Silver, Black Back	Anything that swims and eats baitfish
Tomlin	Johnson Sprint Spoon	Gold ½ ounce	Anything in the area I fish
Van Horn	RipTide Mullet	Red/White	Just about anything that swims
Wiggins	D.O.A. C.A.L. Shad Tail	Electric Chicken	Reds, Trout, about anything else

Note: Master anglers use their favorite lures in different sizes depending on conditions. The most common weight reported is

½ ounce. Many anglers also believe that contrast and silhouettes may be more important than color.

Bringing Them to the Boat

The Art of Fighting a Fish

Light-tackle fishing is great sport. Given today's technology and the improved rods, reels, and line available to anglers, large fish can be taken on small equipment. Both from the standpoint of skill and conservation, there are many things to learn from Florida's master anglers.

Don't forget that the notion of light tackle is relative. If you are fishing for 150-pound tarpon, 15-pound tackle is light. If you are fishing for 7-pound trout, 2-pound tackle is light. You always want to match your tackle to the fish that you target.

Hooking a fish is one thing, but successfully landing and releasing a big fish is another. If you don't want to ever say again, "The big one got away," read on for more tips to bring the big one to the boat.

Pre-Fishing Tips

Completing a successful catch and release, or catching an evening dinner, starts long before you have a fish on the hook. Capt. Rick Grassett prepares for each trip by making sure he has the appropriate-size tackle on board for the fish he expects to encounter. He always inspects his mainline and terminal connections—line to leader and leader to lure, respectively. Also, in the case he hooks a large fish, he makes sure to have a fighting belt and gloves on board.

Begin by checking your line, leader, and knots. If you find a frayed or worn leader, replace it. In fact, it is not a bad idea to routinely begin a day's fishing with a fresh leader. Many master anglers who use monofilament line start every day with a fresh spool of mainline. By replacing the mainline or the leader you are forced to retie the knots as well. If you replace the mainline-to-leader knot and the knot to the hook or lure, you increase your chances of landing a trophy fish. At least, in this scenario, you are starting with the strongest possible links between you and the fish to come.

Capt. Ray Markham's pre-fishing checklist includes the regular check of tackle, weather, wind direction and velocity, radar, tide levels and changes, and solunar periods. Then he checks the obvious, "Gas in the boat, battery charges, and before I leave the dock, I always check the bilge pump."

Capt. "Bouncer" Smith states his notion of rigging in plain English. "I always rig tackle like we may catch a world record—that includes proper leader size and length. I use dependable chemically sharpened hooks but still check them to be sure they are sharp. I always keep the reels full of quality line that is in good condition. That means checking often for nicks, cuts, and abrasions."

Big cobia can be taken on light tackle but not without good knots and equipment that are in good working order.

Capt. Troy Mell also reminds anglers about the importance of sharp hooks. A dull hook simply doesn't have the same chance of ending up in a fish's mouth. Captain Mell says, "Make sure the hooks are sharp. Sometimes I sharpen them even when they are fresh out of the box." You should also be sure the eyes are completely closed. A hook with an open eye can mean disaster on a big fish capable of pulling the leader through the gap in the eye. It doesn't happen often, but when you are targeting big fish you should check the eye and close it with a pair of pliers if necessary.

Anglers should also check their reel for loose or worn parts that may fail during a fight with a trophy fish. It is really better to perform this check after the previous fishing trip, before you store your reel. This is also a good time to add lubrication to vital moving parts that make your reel perform smoothly. Capt. Richard Grathwohl reminds anglers not to forget the line roller on the spinning reel, make

sure that it rolls freely and doesn't stick. If it's not operating correctly, he says it will result in a lost fish for sure. Reel maintenance
can be easily overlooked in the rush to get home at the end of the
day, and it could result in a lost fish the next time out. Just keep the
maintenance simple, don't overlubricate and use light petroleum-
based oil, unless your manufacturer specifically calls for grease in
a certain location. Most reels come with an owner's manual, which
gives complete maintenance tips and lubrication points. When you
are hooked up with a big one you don't want your reel to fail.

One of the most important aspects of the reel is the drag. This is
because it is intended to allow you to fight a big fish without breaking your line or terminal connections. You should check your drag
before each fishing trip and set it appropriate to the size of line you
are using. During the maintenance routine, you should tighten
the drag to be sure it is possible to create a good deal of resistance
against the mainline as it is pulled from the spool. At the other extreme, be sure that the drag will loosen to the point where there is
hardly any drag at all. Various fishing situations will require a wide
range of drag settings, and you want to be sure you can obtain all
levels—from light drag to tight drag. If your reel will not accomplish
this wide range, you should inspect the drag washers to see if they
need to be replaced.

Experienced anglers learn to set their drag by feel, but in the early
stages of acquiring this skill, it is wise to use a small scale, which are
commercially available just for the job, or you may use a small fish
scale. Run the mainline through the guides on the rod and pull an
additional five to six feet beyond the last guide. Tie a loop on the
end of the line. Attach the loop to the hook on the scale. This will
allow you to measure the pull you place on the line while adjusting
the drag. Secure the rod in a vise or have someone hold it horizontally. Most manufacturers recommend setting the drag at about
30 percent of the mainline's breaking strength. This means that if
the mainline is 20-pound test, the drag should be set at about six
pounds pull. When the reading on the scale is six pounds, the line
should barely be coming off the spool. As you raise the rod tip, as

you would to fight a fish, the bend in the rod will increase the drag, and line will not come off at the six-pound setting.

The measured drag will also increase as line is taken off the spool. For example, if a big fish takes half the line from your spool, the diameter of the remaining line on the spool is smaller and the amount of pull needed to take off more line is increased. This is where you need to be careful on a really big fish, because you may begin pushing beyond the stated breaking strength of the line. Fish such as tarpon and big ocean jacks can break you off with another hard run. This would be a good time to loosen up the drag a bit to avoid the break off. Fish such as kingfish often make that initial long run but wear out doing it. It is not as likely that you would need to loosen the drag in this scenario.

When fishing with light tackle, the angler may want to set the drag on the light side and finger or palm the spool to add drag. Captain Mell says, "Have the drag a little lighter than normal. A finger to the spool can add drag when the fish runs, but it can be removed in an instant if needed." He adds a final caveat, "Keep your rod tip up and never let slack in the line. Don't rush it."

Capt. Ed "Jazz" Jazwierski has a place on his center console where he places the hook and pulls back on the rod to check how much tension it takes for his drag to pay out, making any adjustments as needed. He has developed this procedure over time and does not need a scale to get the tension he wants. With practice, most anglers are able to accomplish this same thing without a scale. One of Captain Jazz's favorite targets is snook, and he has a tip for fishing snook on the beach. "When beach fishing for snook, I do tend to have a lighter setting for my drag, since the fish are on the larger size and there are few obstructions, the fish can run a little easier and I'm able to palm the spool when needed to quickly get the fish in."

The main thing with drags is to set them correctly at the beginning of the day, and check them often during the day. Also, know your fish and what to expect of them, so you can make adjustments if needed. Drag settings also depend on how you are fishing. Capt. Troy Mell says, "With topwater lures, I back off on the drag, because the hook up is less solid and I don't want to pull the hooks. On the other hand, if fishing close to structure, I tighten down on plastics so I can turn the fish away from a possible break off."

During a fight with a hefty fish, your line, leader, and knots are strained, and hooks may be slowly straightening. A properly set drag can prevent the mainline, leader, knots, or hooks from failing.

Fish On

If you are fishing with a guide and hook up with a big one, you are likely to get some friendly advice on how to land the fish. Professional guides have been there, done that, and can advise you on the proper techniques that turn dreams into reality. Captain Grassett says, "Depending on the client's experience, I may need to coach them along so they don't make novice mistakes. With experienced anglers, my attention is turned to boat handling." Professional fishing guides are willing teachers, and there is no better place to learn the finer points of fishing.

"When you have a big fish at boatside, focus on the landing and not on anything that may take your mind off the fish," says Capt. Pat Dineen. "Clear the clutter off the deck and prevent anything interfering with the landing of the fish." Captain Dineen coaches anglers to close the gap between the rod and the fish as soon as possible, "This allows you to keep track of the fish's head so you can always pull toward the tail. Continue to apply maximum pressure throughout the fight—increase drag by palming the spool and respond to a fish's surge by releasing the spool."

Short of setting the hook, Capt. Robert McCue says, the next most important thing in fighting a fish is a bent rod. "A bent rod is a tight line. Often a shallow hooked fish, or even a fish that is not hooked well at all, will be landed if the line is tight. Novice anglers have a tendency to use the reel to fight a fish instead of the rod. The angler should bend the rod with muscle and then store the line on the reel by dropping the rod and reeling."

A bent rod lets the fish know who is in charge. Captain McCue says big-game fish such as tarpon or structure-orientated fish such

Bent rods mean tight lines. You may need to change angle or pressure, but always keep the rod bent when landing a fish.

as snook need to be fought with a psychological edge against the fish. "Often when you break the will or confuse a fish, it tends to give up quicker, or turns away from the structure it was orientated to." He reminds us that drags are designed to slow down fish and then pay line out of the spool, not land them.

With bigger fish and potentially longer fights, Captain McCue says you have to change the angle of pressure but always keep the rod bent. You want to make the fish work for every inch of line it takes from your reel. "With a proper drag setting, the fish cannot break your line—short of bad line, knots, contact with structure, or chewing through the leader. Your goal should be to beat its psychological will and animal instinct to resist and survive. Beat it mentally, and you will win physically. Some finesse is required on soft-mouthed fish such as trout, but keep the pressure in perspective to the species and strength of the fish, and the landing technique is the same."

Captain McCue continues, "Fight them hard, and put all of the tackle to the test. This is a fight—you against the beast. Fight hard, change your angles, try to put him on his back, and confuse him. A fish has never been on his back, so do that or try to; you will work harder, but not as long. The faster and harder you fight, the faster the fish will come to you, leaving less time for something else to go wrong."

A similar forceful approach is taken by Capt. Tom Van Horn. "I like to fight my fish aggressively and keep its head turned to me as much as possible. I typically fish with fifteen- to twenty-pound-test braid with my drag set at about six-pounds tension, approximately one-third the breaking strength of the line. As I get closer to the end of the fight, I will tighten up the drag to increase the tension on the fish as it grows weaker."

According to Capt. Dave Sutton, the most important thing about fish fights is the angle of your line in relation to the fish. "Your line must be over the fish's back to maintain the hook set. Another important tactic is to keep steady pressure on the fish during the runs and head shakes, as the fight continues. Keeping a steady bend in the rod while a fish runs, jumps, zigs, and zags is an art form and should be practiced on every fish whether it's the big one or not."

Captain Sutton also suggests letting the fish determine the length of the fight. "All five-pound redfish are not the same just like all one-hundred-eighty-pound people are not the same. Some are just plain mean, while others are not. Do not hurry a fish to the boat. Enjoy the fight and keep steady pressure on the fish while it expends its energy, not yours." Captain Sutton says the fish will tell the angler when it is ready to be brought to the boat by rolling over on its side on the surface. This is when it's safe to slowly lead it to the boat or shore for capture. He also warns anglers to never lift a fish with the rod and always keep pressure on the fish during the landing, just in case he has a little life left and makes that final run from the boat. Following a few simple steps in landing your fish will result in more photos to record your memories and to show to your friends.

When a fish rolls over on its side at the surface, it's time to bring it toward the boat for release.

Captain Jazz says his mind starts racing when he, or more likely, a client has a big fish on. He says questions come to mind such as, "Is the line tight? Where is the fish in relation to the structure? Is the fish taking off for the mangroves, dock piling, crab trap, or out in the open? Is the line straight to the fish or wrapped around something because the fish is running for cover? What direction is the fish heading? Do I need to move so I have a better angle to keep the fish from wrapping around or going under something?" Responding to these questions often makes the difference between a successful catch and release or another one that got away. If you are the angler in this situation, let your fishing partners know what they can do to help you land your trophy fish.

Captain Markham says lots of things flash through his mind when an angler on his boat has a fish on. In addition to the questions above, he adds a tip related to catching another fish while you already have one on. If it's a trout, for example, the question becomes, "Are there other trout with it?" He says, "Multiple hookups are possible if you cast near a fish being reeled in slowly." Remember, this is not a technique to use when one angler has a trophy fish on. In that case all other anglers should bring in their lines and full attention should go to the angler with the big fish.

Along with every other master angler, Captain Jazz says, "Never reel against the drag when the fish is taking line and the drag is screaming. Let the fish run, do not reel. When the fish stops, the angler should start reeling. By reeling against the drag you may snap the line with the added tension, or at the least, put twists in the line that will make a mess on your next cast."

There are times when a fish is taking drag and headed to the mangroves or other structure where the threat of cutting off looms. In such cases, Captain Jazz suggests palming the spool for added pressure. You have to take the risk, try to turn the fish away from the potential hazard. "If the line snaps that's okay, it was going to break you off anyway."

Captain Bouncer has another tip for when fish are running for cover and your tackle is relatively light. "If a fish is unstoppable and running for pilings or mangrove trees that might cut your line, open your bail or free spool your reel. The fish will frequently stop when the sudden lack of pressure leads them to think they have escaped." This tactic may be just what the angler needs to get the fish swimming in the opposite direction and become a photo op instead of a broken line. The same tactic will sometimes work even after a big fish has wrapped you on some type of structure. If you have the patience to open the bail it will remove tension from the fish and give them a few minutes to calm down. Sometimes the fish will swim right back out, the same way it went in. On a trophy fish, it's worth the try.

Captain Bouncer also reminds anglers to point the rod at the fish when it surges away, either on a long run or at the last minute near the boat. This will help eliminate breakoffs, because when the rod is pointed upward, the combined drag of the reel and the rod is stron-

Even a small angler can land a big fish with proper rod techniques. Once a stalemate is reached, short pumps of the rod will aid the angler in gaining line.

ger than the drag itself, and chances of breaking a line or pulling a hook increases.

When fighting a big fish, such as a tarpon or big redfish, Capt. Keith Kalbflesich instructs his anglers to never hold the rod higher than eleven o'clock and never lower than parallel to the water, until the fish is near the boat. Keep maximum pressure on the fish at all times and always pull toward the tail. If you follow this strategy, it will starve the fish of oxygen, shorten the fight, and keep the hook solid in the corner of the mouth.

Captain Kalbflesich says the angler should maintain tension on the fish at a level where the drag is either slipping or line is being placed back on the spool by turning the reel handle. Once a stalemate is reached, where no line is going out or coming in, the angler should start short pumps of the rod from level to about ten o'clock. These pumps should be slow and deliberate, while placing line back on the spool by cranking the reel handle and dropping the rod parallel to the water. Captain Kalbflesich gives a mental image of the process, "It's like trying to lift a bucket of sand without breaking the line or allowing the drag to slip."

Capt. Chris Myers says, "If a big fish is not taking line off the reel, you should be getting it back. Never let them rest." This technique wears a fish down quickly. I have seen Captain Myers bring big tarpon and other big fish to boatside quickly, because he constantly applies maximum pressure.

Captain Markham agrees. If you are fighting a tarpon, the fish needs to be boatside in less than thirty minutes or the fish goes free. "Maximum pressure needs to be applied to the fish to break his spirit and land him quickly." Tarpon are too important to sportfishing to kill them, and that is exactly what happens if the fight goes on too long.

Sometimes a fish will run under the boat. Then, the angler should respond by sticking the rod tip into the water far enough to avoid a trolling motor on the bow or a main engine on the stern. Keep the rod tip in the water and work your way around the boat to the side the fish is on. Captain Jazz says this is another reason to use long rods. "Longer rods aid in fighting fish. If a fish goes under the boat, you are able to stick the tip farther into the water with a long rod, clearing the line of the bottom of the vessel, trolling motor, or main engine propeller."

The position of the boat is another important factor in fighting big fish. Captain Grassett turns his attention to boat handling when his client is hooked up to a trophy-size fish that requires everything to be done right in order to land it. Captain Mell agrees. One of the first things he thinks about when a client gets on a big fish is boat position. "If the boat is in a bad position, the client may lose the fish right off the bat. I try to keep the fish in front of the boat so I can see the line and what the angler is doing; if some coaching is needed it is simple to do."

Boat-handling techniques include keeping the boat downwind or downcurrent of the fish when possible. If you are chasing a big fish like a tarpon to regain line, the boat should never travel faster than you can wind line while still placing maximum pressure on the fish. When the angler has control and is bringing the fish toward the boat, the engine should be in neutral and the captain ready to respond to the fish's next move. The angler has the main responsibility for the fight, but a skilled captain can increase the possibility of landing a really big fish.

Just as the term *light tackle* is relative to the size of the fish you catch, the term *big fish* is relative to the species of fish you target. Different species require different techniques to land. At the other extreme from tarpon, a five-pound or larger trout is a big fish, relative to the species. However, you do not use the same techniques to land spotted sea trout that you do to land tarpon. Sea trout have a very soft mouth and a large opening can tear around the hook. Captain Markham says, "The larger the fish, the more carefully you need to play the fish to the boat and the tighter the line and bend in the rod needs to be maintained." When targeting soft-mouthed trout, Captain Markham uses a fast-action rod with a soft tip that allows him to apply a soft but constant pressure to the fish as it is brought to the boat. The constant pressure prevents the hook from falling out of the tear that is likely to develop in the fish's mouth, and the soft tip doesn't pull the hook completely.

What Not to Do

While it is important to learn the various techniques for properly landing fish, it is also important to understand some of the things you should not do. When asked what not to do while fighting a fish, Captain Markham said that a failure to keep the line tight is probably the worst thing an angler can do. Other things on his list include, "Tightening the drag, reeling against the drag, pointing the rod at the fish, reeling the fish all the way up to the rod tip, and trying to lift the fish into the boat with the rod." He also warns anglers not to high-stick the rod once the fish is near or in the boat.

High-sticking occurs when an angler raises the rod above the proper fighting angle and can, when taken far enough, result in a broken rod. Rods are not designed to take the pressure in that direction. Unfortunately, high sticking is something that could happen easily to inexperienced anglers, because it normally occurs as the fish gets close to the boat and excitement and anticipation of landing the fish causes a loss of concentration.

If you think a large fish is going to spool you, Captain Van Horn says, "Do not tighten the drag. As the line feeds off your reel, the extra weight of the line will add drag without you doing anything. The best thing to do is put your rod in the rod holder and let the fish pull away. Once it stops or turns back, lift the rod and start reeling again; let the rod do the work."

Another action to avoid is dropping the rod tip too quickly when pumping on a big fish. If an angler drops the rod tip too quickly, slack line is created at the rod tip. If the tip is then pulled back up through the slack, there is a possibility of wrapping the slack around the tip of the rod. If this wrap occurs, the drag is disabled and the angler cannot retrieve the line. A big fish is likely to break the line or pull the hook under these conditions.

Captain Jazz agrees with the school of thought that says, the worse thing an angler can do is let the fish have slack in the line. He says, "Always keep the line tight with a bend in the rod. The only time you should have slack in the line is when you have a tarpon on and must "bow to the king." When a tarpon jumps, stop reeling and point the rod tip at the fish. This will keep the hook from pulling out of a tarpon's mouth on the jump when they gain leverage with a tight line. A tarpon's mouth is very hard and boney; there are only a few spots a hook can really sink in. Don't horse the fish in, because more often than not, you will lose the fish to a broken line or rip the hook out of the fish's mouth. Captain Jazz says, "I see it all the time."

Landing Nets

Anglers who want to keep their catch for the dinner table often use landing nets to bring the fish aboard the boat. It is probably the most efficient way to remove the fish from the water without taking a chance on losing it. The majority of these landing nets are made with a knotted mesh design. These nets work fine to land the fish, but have the drawback of easily entangling your hooks as well as your fish, especially if you use artificial lures containing treble hooks. All mesh nets can be a real pain when the hooks become entangled. An alternative to the old-style knotted mesh is now available.

New tangle-free rubber netting is becoming more popular among both catch-and-release anglers and those who want to keep their catch. The nets work just as efficiently as the older styles, plus they give the added advantage of resisting hook penetration and reducing the time involved with removing an entangled fish from the net. The new rubber nets also tend to protect the fish's coating of slime, which helps keep it from bacterial infection. Old-style nets are more likely to remove that protective coating and lessen the fish's chances of recovery when released.

Remember, even if you do want to keep some fish for dinner, you still catch a lot of fish that have to be returned to the water. You can invest in a rubber-mesh net, just for the conservation aspect it provides and also enjoy the hook-resistant feature that will give you more fishing time. The new rubber nets come in all sizes, so choose the one that fits the fish you catch most often.

Release Methods

Today's fishing regulations require anglers to release fish that may have been kept legally only a few years ago. For any fish that must be released, the angler's goal should be to release them alive.

Overplaying a fish until it's really exhausted will more than likely kill the fish, so try to land them in a reasonable period of time. If you don't take time to revive a landed fish before releasing it, the fish will not have much of a chance for survival. A released fish may swim away from you, but if not properly revived, may die later. Captain Jazz says, "Run around the block five times, no stopping, and then hold your breath. That's what you do to a fish when you take it out of the water at the end of the fight. Carefully release the fish you don't

Released fish sometimes turn on their side and float or sink to the bottom; when they do, you should retrieve the fish and start the resuscitation process over again.

plan to keep. *Do not* use a towel for handling; it takes off the fish's protective slime coating." By not removing the protective slime that fights bacteria and by returning the fish to the water quickly, the possibility of the fish living increases dramatically.

Captain Jazz continues, "Quickly unhook the fish and return it to the water, holding it until recovered." Recovered means the fish can keep itself upright with its side fins and tail moving. If you let a fish go and it starts to lean to one side and sink toward the bottom, the fish is not yet ready to be released. Recapture the fish when this happens and start the process all over again. When the water is warmer, this process of revival may take longer, but it needs to be done. Captain Jazz says, "You spent all that time trying to catch the fish, take the time to revive it, watch it swim away for someone else to catch, and allow it to produce more fish for the future."

Often, as hard as you try, released fish will still die after apparently swimming off in good shape. Marine scientists report that about 2 percent of snook are likely to die after being released. About 5 percent of redfish and 8 percent of spotted sea trout meet the same unwanted fate.

Proper handling is the first thing anglers should consider when a fish is to be released. Simply wetting your hands before handling a fish can improve the chances of a live release. Another simple tactic of many of Florida's master anglers is to crush the barbs on their hooks. They often do this when they are enjoying their personal fishing time, but may not when fishing with clients. For many master anglers, crushing the barbs is a conservation technique that allows most fish to be removed from the hook easier while increasing the chance of survival. Captain Myers says, "I bend the barbs down on all the hooks I fish with personally. On most charters, I do not." Many people are very skeptical of barbless-hook fishing and inexperienced with landing fish. If the angler will keep a tight line to the fish at all times, a fish won't be lost because the barb is bent down. Captain Myers says, "Inexperienced anglers have a tendency to allow slack to get into the line, and that can allow a barbless hook to fall out. I use barbless hooks because it makes releasing the fish much easier."

Captain Jazz echoes this advice. "As long as the angler keeps a bend in the rod, the hook will stay in the fish. What I find with most beginners is they lower the rod tip too fast, and they're not reeling down smoothly and keeping a bend in the rod. That slack in the line is enough to let the hook fall out. The fish swims off, and you're left empty handed. As you lower the rod tip, keep reeling. Be smooth, take your time." He adds, "It's so much easier to release the fish when the barbs are bent down, and if you should get one in your finger or somewhere worse, it comes right out and you keep fishing, instead

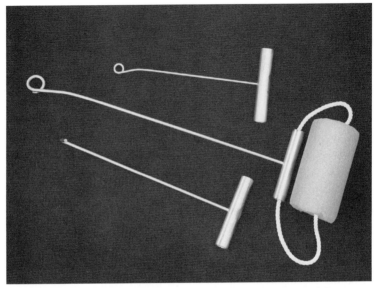

The ARC dehooker comes in different sizes and designs to fit the fish you target. Attach a float to the dehooker in case you lose it overboard.

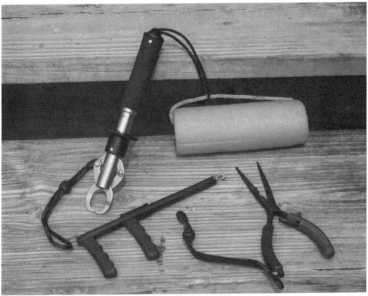

Long-nose pliers, pistol-grip dehookers, and BogaGrip fish handlers are great tools for handling and releasing big fish.

of making a trip to the hospital where some guy in a white coat will ruin a perfectly good hook."

There are also good dehooking devices available on the market to ease the task of removing the hook from the fish. The one I use on my boat is an ARC dehooker. With this simple dehooking device, I can remove either circle or J-hooks without ever touching the fish. They come in different sizes and designs to fit the fish that you target. Using this tool will allow more of your released fish to live to fight another day.

If you bring a fish to the boat and see that the hook is deep in the mouth, not in the lip, you simply place the pigtail of the dehooker over the line and rotate it one-quarter turn, leaving the line inside the pigtail. Pull up on the leader and push down on the tool until it is bottomed out in the curve of the hook. At this point, a downward thrust on the tool will normally remove the hook and secure it alongside the pigtail as the tool is pulled from the fish's mouth.

If the fish is hooked externally, repeat the process described above until you have the pigtail settled in the curve of the hook. At this point, grasp the leader firmly and begin to rotate the leader downward and the dehooker upward. Apply enough pressure to keep the leader and the dehooker in a straight line. As you move toward a vertical position, with the tool handle up and leader held down, you will observe the fish's own weight beginning to pull against the hook, and it will quickly dislodge. The fish will fall back into the water without ever being touched by the angler.

Other handy tools for removing fish hooks include long-nosed pliers, pistol-grip hook removers, and BogaGrip fish handlers. The BogaGrip provides a means for gripping the fish, while using one of the other tools to remove the hook.

Last Cast

Recent scientific evidence concludes that it is extremely stressful to hang a fish vertically from a holding device or, for that matter, from your hand. Holding a fish in this vertical position, especially for big heavy fish, is said to cause internal organ damage. The best release

If you want to take a photo of your catch, support the fish horizontally and return it to the water as quickly as possible.

technique for any fish is to leave it in the water while removing the hook. If the hook cannot be easily removed, cut the leader as close to the hook as possible, and let Mother Nature take care of removing the hook. The increased trauma, associated with a struggle to remove the hook, is likely to do more damage and decrease the fish's chance of survival.

If you must remove the fish from the water for a photo, carefully cradle the fish or support it in a horizontal position. Take the photo as quickly as possible and return the fish to the water. Every successful release today multiplies the opportunity to have more fish in the future.

9

The Golden Rule

Good Manners for the Angler

The only ripples on the water were those made by a school of redfish eating their way down the flat. The calm wind, blue sky, and perfect sunlight had set up conditions that all flats anglers dream of. The big motor had been turned off as the boat left the channel and the distance to the shallow water had been closed by poling the skiff almost to within casting distance of the school of reds. The adrenaline rush was high, and the anglers were ready, when in the distance, an engine could be heard coming in the direction of the flat. The fishermen expected the boat's engine to shut down, but that did not occur, and the inconsiderate angler motored up on the flat and blew out the fishing for everyone.

With all the information available about how to fish, when to fish, and where to fish, there are many such examples that indicate anglers don't know how or don't care how they behave when they fish around other people. In my mind, good sportsmanship and conservation demand that anglers should also possess knowledge about how to conduct themselves on the water.

The Golden Rule, when applied to angling, gives us guidance when it comes to respecting other anglers. The Golden Rule is a simple moral principle that, in fishing terminology, says all anglers should treat other anglers as he or she would like to be treated in return. Good fishing etiquette is as simple as thoughtful application of the Golden Rule to other anglers, managing the environment, and protecting the fishery resource. Practices such as obeying the laws, handling released fish properly, participating in fisheries management, and simply being considerate to other fishermen will accrue great benefits. Additionally, all of us are role models to the younger generation of anglers. Teaching proper fishing etiquette to kids will encourage them to develop a sense of caring and appreciation for our fisheries resources.

Respecting the Rights of Others

Capt. Chris Myers identified the one principle of ethical angling that gets violated most often. "The most common violation of fishing etiquette that I see is that other anglers often drive too close to where other people are fishing and spook the fish with their motor." This same notion was identified time and time again in the interviews with the guides represented in this book.

According to Capt. Blair Wiggins, an unethical angler once ran a flat between Captain Wiggins's boat and the shoreline. Captain Wiggins was poling along, following a school of redfish, when another boat came running up the flat along the shoreline in an attempt to bump a school of reds. The result was rather obvious. The possibility of Captain Wiggins's clients catching any of these redfish were gone, because of one mindless angler. He attempted to respectfully explain to the other angler how they could work together, but that resulted in a shouting match with words that Captain Wiggins says can't be mentioned in this book. "If this angler wanted to find redfish without burning the flats, I would have been happy to teach him. He would have been better off being open-minded, rather than closed-minded to the situation."

Capt. Tom Van Horn had a similar incident on Mosquito Lagoon. He was staked out on a school of redfish when another guide boat, with clients, approached the flat on plane. The approaching boat shut down within fifty feet of Captain Tom's boat, dropped his trolling motor, and proceeded to push the school of reds away. The other boat came so close that it picked up an angler's line in his trolling motor. Captain Van Horn's client asked, "What should I do about the fishing line peeling off my reel?" Captain Van Horn replied, "Open the bail, I need new line anyway."

In cases such as this, proper fishing etiquette is relatively simple. A second or third boat should never come in on another boat unless invited in. "In our area," says Captain Van Horn, "the larger schools of redfish are often fished by more than one boat, as long as they are all playing together on the same game card."

Captain Myers agrees and adds this advice. "When fishing in close quarters, as when several boats are on a school of big redfish, anglers should take turns allowing the other boats a chance at the fish instead of everyone going at them all at once." This is one of those times when good etiquette can actually result in more fish for everyone. These fish would be less likely to get spooked and disappear if the opportunity is shared among the anglers instead of being attacked from all sides.

When another boat operates between his fishing lines and the shoreline, Capt. Dale Fields says that just a little more effort by the other boat captain could eliminate a potential problem. "If it was necessary for the other boat to take a shortcut between me and the shoreline, he could just ask permission or at least offer an explanation as to why he had to interfere with my fishing. When boats run shallow-water flats, it disturbs a large area and shuts the fishing down for everybody fishing in that vicinity." Captain Fields says the solution is simple, "Just don't do it. However, it is difficult to tell someone the advantages of working together when all you can see is a rooster tail from their prop." Yet, education is the answer, however it might be provided.

An ethical and caring angler should simply heed the advice of Captain Myers. He says, "Take time to drive around other anglers fishing the flats. In the grand scheme, it only takes you a few seconds or minutes more and can prevent another angler's chances of catching fish from being ruined."

If there are enough fish to go around, an ethical angler may wave or motion another boat into the area. If the invitation comes, the new boat should pole or quietly and slowly enter the area with the trolling motor on a constant slow speed. Turn off live wells and other mechanical devices that cause noise, and join the fun. Your consideration of the situation and your knowledge of how to approach it will improve the fishing experiences for everyone.

Capt. Pat Dineen says this notion of ethical angling all boils down to treating others as you would expect to be treated. He says for his area, fishing etiquette issues often revolve around stalking tarpon on the move or staking out for tarpon in shallow water and letting them come to you. "The key is to provide plenty of room. If someone pulls up on a shoreline ahead of you, in the direction you are poling, then you may as well quit fishing and go elsewhere. Similarly, someone who stakes out on the same line as you to the east—when the tarpon are migrating from east to west—eliminates or severely reduces the number of casts to passing fish and the likelihood of you jumping a fish." In the end, it's all about consideration of others and using common sense. The last thing we need is an outbreak of boat rage on the flats.

Capt. Richard Grathwohl states this crowding problem in terms of simple respect. "It used to be common law among anglers to come in behind another angler already on the flat." He thinks that too many of today's anglers have lost personal respect for the other guy and have lost the notion of sharing a flat and the fish on it. "Many anglers think they own the flat and to heck with anyone else."

Captain Grathwohl sees the problem as one that has developed over the years. More fishing pressure, by more and more anglers, has resulted in too many bad apples in the barrel. Using common courtesy and a mindset of teamwork would go a long way toward making everyone's fishing experience a better one.

Another unethical practice that is becoming too common in the Keys involves anglers who hold their position with a push pole, instead of staking out. They wait for a school of fish to come down the bank, push them out off the bank, and work the school. This practice eliminates the chance of another boat getting a shot at them. Too often, when they finish with that school, they pole back up on the bank, where they wait to cut out another school and fish it by themselves. Captain Grathwohl says if you approach them and ask them to show a little respect, they just fire back with "Who are you, and do you think you own the water?"

This growing attitude of not caring and not sharing is a sad statement about some of today's anglers. This behavior leaves the ethical anglers, who try to fish with respect for others, little hope for change. Unfortunately, Captain Myers speaks for many when he says, "I feel there is little that can be done in many of these situations, because saying something to the person usually gets little result."

As far as a solution to this growing problem, Captain Grathwohl says, "I find myself just trying not to get into this mess anymore. I push off the flat and tell my anglers there are too many places to fish to put up with this anymore—and off I go."

For the rest of us there is and needs to be a sense of caring and respect for other anglers similar to what Captain Grathwohl exhibits. "When I see a recreational angler, I treat him with respect, so he will go home and say, 'Those guides in the Keys are all right by me.' Then, I expect the same respect, so we get away from that behavior of every angler for himself." Teaching by example is a powerful tool that can result in improved fishing experiences for all anglers.

On crowded flats, Capt. Ron Tomlin suggests that proper distance should be maintained between boats. He says, "A respectful angler would maintain a minimum of a quarter mile separation and preferably out of sight." Using this visual rule of crowding, respectful anglers would attempt to keep out of sight of other anglers, if possible. "Courtesy on the water is tantamount to safety. If every fisherman will practice the Golden Rule, everyone will have more fun."

Another situation too often encountered is when one angler considers a particular area his private spot and doesn't think anyone else should fish it. This happened to Captain Van Horn with unimaginable consequences. As Captain Van Horn was fishing, he was approached by a possessive angler who commenced to run tight circles around the Van Horn boat, disrupting any chance of catching a fish from that location.

Captain Van Horn says, "This never should have happened." In this particular case the other angler was a guide. "The point I'm trying to make is that guides should be required to maintain a higher standard, and they should be punished for improper behavior by the loss of their licenses."

Guides are looked upon as role models on the water, and what they do is copied by other anglers. Captain Van Horn says the public will translate unethical behavior to a perception that says, "If it is okay for the guides to do it, it must be ok. We need to offset such a perception by treating other anglers with the same level of respect that we expect." Fishermen who behave badly, as in this example, may not be capable of doing the right thing, and we will probably have to put up with them in the future, but the rest of us still need to behave in an ethical manner and set good examples that encourage ethical angling.

Capt. Ray Markham agrees that anglers fishing too close to other anglers can spoil the fishing for everyone. "The flats are big," he says, "and no one owns a location. If they think there is only one place that holds fish, they aren't much of an angler anyway. Simply find areas that other people are not using, and fishing will be better for all."

Keep plenty of room between your boat and other boats that are fishing the same area. Fishing enjoyment and success will be better for everyone.

It can be a little disappointing to motor up to your intended spot and find someone else already there fishing, but it doesn't need to ruin your day. Captain Markham says if this happens to him he simply gives them the water and looks for other opportunities. "If it is an area that must be used in transit to other areas, an ethical angler will come off plane and use the trolling motor to pass, so as to not spook the fish."

Let's face it, anglers who fish in a location that is a navigation route, such as a channel, should expect other anglers to use that channel without regard to fishing. Nevertheless, Captain Markham says, "If there are alternative routes I try to take them, to respect the anglers who are fishing."

Capt. "Bouncer" Smith says anglers should also behave out of respect for other anglers when moving up on a fishing spot to anchor. On one occasion, he was anchored upstream from a wreck and catching yellowtail snapper, when a large sportfishing boat came along and dropped anchor. When the tides and winds were through influencing the final position of the other boat, it ended up 30 feet behind Bouncer's boat and in the chum line. Bouncer reported, "We had a ball pulling three twenty-pound-plus grouper and two fifty-pound plus amberjacks out from under his bow. Of course, he did scare off our yellowtails."

Bouncer obviously made the best of a bad situation, but with respect to ethical angling, the other boat captain was way out of line. According to Bouncer, "An ethical angler would never anchor or fish in another angler's chum line or anchor in the drift of another boat." Finally, he says, "Don't set up in the path of fish swimming toward another boat's bait spread. Always arrive and leave a fishing fleet by slowing before you reach the fleet, and idle away before hitting the throttles." Those simple rules of behavior would eliminate a huge boat wake from affecting other anglers' fishing pleasure, as boats arrive and leave a popular fishing area.

Captain Markham emphasizes the element of noise and how it relates to shallow-water fishing. Noise made on the water, by a boat running too close to another boat on shallow-water flats, should be eliminated when possible. He says, "Noise blows the fishing out for everyone. Stealth and *no motors running* on the flats will make better angling for all." The solution to this problem is so simple, yet many inconsiderate or unknowing anglers can't seem to accomplish it. "Approach the edge of the flat, shut the big motor off, and enter the area either by drifting, poling, or trolling."

Other areas that deserve consideration from anglers are the very early-morning or late-night hours around residential docks and seawalls. Capt. Markham explains, "Being quiet will keep residents from becoming angry at you for fishing around their property. Making noise or decorating their docks, boats, or lines with hooks, lures, or floats is not a good thing. Do not step on their property to retrieve lures or hooks. Make an effort to be more accurate with your casts, and remove lures and hooks from their property when possible."

Sometimes unethical angling behavior occurs between anglers fishing on the same boat. Captain Tomlin says, "I often find that individual fishermen do not understand the etiquette involved in fishing on a boat. Some angler on the stern of the boat will throw toward the bow, crossing lines with the folks on the bow."

Captain Tomlin solves this problem by dividing the boat from stem to stern. He then suggests to each angler where he should cast. The more anglers on a boat, the more difficult it is to keep them in a particular area; but, if they respect each others' space, all will have a better experience, fewer lines will be tangled, and less fishing time will be lost. The angler fishing from the bow can fish in front of the boat and the angler on the stern can fish behind the boat. Everyone else basically needs to cast at right angles to the boat to give maximum distance between the fishing lines.

Shore-bound anglers should also show proper respect for their fellow anglers. Wade fishermen should use all possible effort not to damage fragile vegetation or other bottom structure. Wading is not a very invasive activity, but can still cause minimal damage to the flats. Anglers should, when possible, limit foot traffic by using the shoreline to move from one area to another, as long as it does not violate laws of trespass.

Shore-bound anglers should also be aware that boat-access areas can be busy places. Avoid fishing from boat ramps where you might get in the way of docking boats. It would make more sense to fish in a location that is less congested, since boat activity itself will likely disperse the fish.

Captain Van Horn reported an incident that involved both a shore-bound angler and a boat. "While fishing with clients in Sebastian Inlet, an angler fishing from shore intentionally cast a one-ounce bucktail jig into my boat from the north jetty. I know this was intentional because, before it struck, he yelled out 'I hope you've got your hard hat on.'" In this case, an FWC officer arrested the unethical angler for public endangerment.

Captain Van Horn says fishing etiquette and common sense are important to all anglers, regardless of how and where they fish. Good behavior should be dictated by the circumstances at hand. In this case, a respectful angler could simply wait until the boat drifted past his position, before making the cast.

Prepare your boat for launching before backing down the ramp. A little courtesy goes a long way at the boat ramp.

Boat ramps provide another opportunity for anglers to come in close proximity. Many public ramps consist of only a couple of slots in which to launch, and ethical behavior is highly desirable. Respectful boaters should do all they can to keep congestion around these limited facilities to a minimum. Use common sense to avoid "ramp rage" and conflict with other boaters. It's not just fishermen trying to get on and off the water, it's also all the recreational boaters who use the same facilities.

Environmental Ethics

Environmental ethics refer to those behaviors that apply to taking care of the resource, the environment you are in when fishing, and the environment the fish live in. In other words, environmental ethics are about conservation.

Capt. Dave Sutton has seen more shallow-water grass beds damaged than he likes to contemplate. He says, "Some people will take a shortcut across a flat, not caring or realizing what happens to the grass beds, or the fishing of a nearby boat. There are just too many advertisements proclaiming that some manufacturer's boat will run in twelve inches of water." Needless to say, there are plenty of boaters out there testing the proclamation. Captain Sutton adds, "We all want our own private little fishing spot, but when the engine is on, some people forget just how important that is to everybody else around them." Captain Sutton says some people just don't get it. They buy a big go-fast-in-shallow-water boat and they just have to get out there and try it, without local knowledge of the water.

Much more will be said about the environmental realities of our precious resource from a scientific perspective in Chapter 11, but for now at least we can discuss a few simple things any angler can do in the name of ethical behavior.

Trash and Debris

The simplest of all things we can do is to keep the resource free of trash. It's really not hard to carry out what you carry in. Don't be a litterbug and distribute your trash all over the fishery. If you are like me and most other guides and recreational anglers, you often take out more than you take in. I've picked up discarded rotten cast nets, rigging lines, dip nets, and monofilament and carried it back to the dock to be disposed of properly. Bait buckets, coolers, and shoes have also taken the ride to the trash bin.

It's not because I am a neat freak, but I do oppose the visual pollution that results from uncaring anglers who dispose their trash in our waterways. Additionally, I do not enjoy finding a dead bird with someone's discarded monofilament line wrapped around it, which prevented it from flying and feeding, thereby leading to its death. We all need to do our part. Wouldn't you rather enjoy a clean, litter-free shoreline, as opposed to one cluttered with trash and debris?

Shallow-Water Ethics

Ethical anglers should respect the fragile shallow-water system that is common to Florida fishing. Many species of marine life are dependent upon the health and well-being of sea grass and other marine plants found in these shallow waters. The vegetation serves as nurseries for juvenile fish, while at the same time providing needed nutrients for their growth.

In order to protect and promote the health of these vital habitats, anglers should always be mindful of the depth of the water and be sure their prop does not come in contact with the bottom. Prop contact is sure to cause scarring and damage to marine plants and organisms, and reduce the ability of the flats to support the very fish we wish to perpetuate.

If the water is too shallow for main power, switch over to a trolling motor or use a push pole. When the winds are favorable you can set up a drift and accomplish your objective without causing any harm to the environment. Approaching all shallow-water fishing areas with caution may even yield improved fishing results to the ethical angler, because the stealthy approach is less likely to spook the fish and it will certainly be better for the habitat.

Laws and Regulations

Fishing laws and regulations are made to protect and conserve the resource. It is each angler's responsibility to know and understand the laws related to the particular fishing they do; it is also their responsibility to report resource violations to the proper authorities.

The laws in Florida are enforced by the marine patrol officers of the Florida Fish and Wildlife Conservation Commission (FWC). Most of the officers are sworn personnel and fully constituted police officers, as provided under Florida Statute 372.07. This designation gives them the authority to enforce all of the laws of the state of Florida, not just the ones related to resource violations.

The FWC Web site reports that its officers provide protection and enforcement of laws related to all wild-animal and aquatic resources in the state. Their enforcement duties include 672 species of wildlife, 208 species of freshwater fish, and more than 500 species of saltwater fish.

The officers on patrol face a daunting challenge of covering 37 million acres of public and private land, 8,246 miles of tidal coastline, 12,000 miles of rivers and streams, 300,000 acres of lakes and ponds, and 11,000 miles of canals. Reading these statistics certainly

Rules and regulations don't always make sense but still must be obeyed.
Sometimes it's simply an issue of safety.

suggest why anglers should help by reporting resources violations
when they see them.

The FWC provides several hotlines for reporting resource violations. In case of a marine emergency or to report resource violations
you can call 1-888-404-3922. Other specific hotlines are available on
the FWC's Web site. Don't take a "let the other guy do it" attitude
when it comes to reporting resources violations. The dedicated officers charged with protecting our precious resources can use all the
help they can get.

Size and Bag Limits

Two of the first regulations that come to mind for most anglers are
size and bag limits on fish. Captain Dineen speaks for most anglers
when he says, "With respect to regulations and bag limits, I am an
ardent supporter and adhere strictly to them. But, if a fish is in sea-

Measured with
Mouth Closed

Total Length

Pinch the Tail

Fish-length measurements are taken from the most forward point of the head, with the mouth closed, to the farthest tip of the tail, with the tail compressed.

son, of legal length, and my customer or I want to bring it home and eat it, it's going home." Captain Dineen's point is that bag limits, seasons, and size restrictions all make sense for the perpetuation of the species, but there is nothing wrong with taking legal fish to be enjoyed on the dining table.

You can visit Florida Wildlife Commission's Web site at http:// myfwc.com/marine/regulation.htm for all the regulations related to seasons, size limits, and how many fish can be legally kept.

The question of legal size depends on the kind of fish you catch and must be determined by measuring in one of two ways. The two methods are total length or fork length measurements.

According to the FWC Web site, the total length is measured from the most forward point of the head, with the mouth closed, to the farthest tip of the tail with the tail compressed or squeezed, while the fish is lying on its side.

Fork length measurements are taken from the tip of the jaw or tip of the snout, with the mouth closed, to the center of the fork in the tail.

Fish regulated by fork length are measured from the tip of the jaw or tip of the snout with closed mouth, to the center of the fork in the tail.

Size limits, along with bag limits, can change from season to season, and it is the angler's responsibility to keep up with these changes. However, just because the bag limit on spotted sea trout is four in the southern region or five in the northern regions doesn't mean that anglers have to keep all trout that are legally permitted. Given the increased fishing pressure being put on Florida's fisheries, more and more anglers are willingly practicing voluntary catch and release; or, at least only taking as many fish as they will use in the next couple of days. Captain Markham says, "While bag and size limits are set by the powers that be, my personal boat limit may be different, and perhaps much more conservative than what is allowed by law."

Captain Markham, as well as many other guides and recreational anglers, recognizes the impact of fishing pressure on the resource and behaves accordingly. It doesn't make much sense to subject the fish to freezer burn and then throw them out at a later date. If anglers truly think of fishing as a sport, there is no need to keep everything that is caught. If you want a memory you can practice CPR (Catch. Photo. Release). In the end, this strategy will result in more fish for everyone to catch, which, after all, is the real joy of fishing.

Last Cast

Good fishing etiquette is as simple as the thoughtful application of the Golden Rule toward other anglers, the fishery resource, and the environment. We anglers can be role models to make the future of the sport more enjoyable for all. Let your vitality and passion for fishing guide others to conduct themselves in positive ways that are beneficial to the sport.

10

Shorten the Learning Curve

How to Hire a Guide

The term "learning curve" refers to the relationship of a person's acquisition and development of skills and behaviors to the time frame in which the skills and behaviors are developed. Applied to fishing, the learning curve can be shortened by hiring a professional fishing guide. Any angler dedicated to learning new skills and behaviors will be well served by engaging the services of one of Florida's many professional fishing guides.

Most of my fishing knowledge was gained by observation and experience. Experience may be the key word here. Fishing knowledge is gained by involvement in the sport of fishing. I was exposed at an early age to fishing. My father took me fishing whenever an opportunity came along. Even today it seems like there is something new to learn each and every time I hit the water. This is especially true if I happen to be fishing with a fellow guide.

Anyone with considerable experience and knowledge in a particular field often gains a reputation as an expert. In the case of the guides contributing to this book, they each qualify many times over as expert anglers. These professional fishing guides are on the water many days a year and have developed countless skills and techniques through their experiences. Can you imagine how much you could learn from them if you were there, with them, on their boat, to observe and ask questions about your particular interests related to fishing? Actually, you may not even have to ask questions. Professional fishing guides are naturally inclined to accommodate their clients and teach them where and how to catch fish. Let's face it, they want you to come back and fish with them again, and they are willing to share their knowledge.

When I visit a new fishing location I often hire a guide, because the first trip to any fishing destination is filled with uncertainty. I expect a guide to relieve some of that uncertainty. When you think about it, hiring a guide can be an economically sound decision. Considering the cost of buying, insuring, maintaining, and storing a boat, and purchasing licenses, bait, and tackle, plus the time required to obtain the local knowledge one needs to catch fish, the cost of a professional guide service is minor. All the client has to do is show up at the dock, board the boat, and fish. They don't even have to bait the hook or take off the fish unless they want to.

Most charter captains provide top-quality tackle and equipment, rigged and ready for fishing. You bring personal items, such as polarized sunglasses, a cap or wide-brim hat, or other convenience items you may want to take. As a courtesy, wear non-scuffing shoes for your charter; black-soled shoes are a no-no. Bring raingear along, not just for the obvious, but for the boat spray from wet rides or extra warmth when needed. If you have medications that will be needed during the day, be sure to bring them, and if you have any special needs of any kind discuss them with your captain.

A cooler with ice and water is normally provided. If you have a favorite beverage you can bring that along. Normally, you can bring your own tackle, but be sure to notify the captain in advance. He may want to leave some of his own tackle at home to have more storage available for yours.

Some charters are catch-and-release only, so no fish are kept. Other charters allow you to harvest fish, but not all of them will clean the fish for you. Occasionally, there are no sufficient facilities for safely cleaning the fish. Under these conditions you are better served to put the fish on ice and clean them when you get to your final destination of the day. Be sure you are clear on expectations about cleaning fish. Either way, you need to bring a cooler to transport your catch back home.

As far as the time frame involved, most guides offer half-day, three-quarter day, or full-day charters that are priced accordingly. For smaller boats the charter prices normally include two anglers. For larger boats the price may include more anglers. Depending on boat capacity, additional anglers can be added for an additional charge. This is an important issue to clarify with your captain. Some captains are willing to charter a half-day trip with the option to extend it, should the client choose to. If you want this option, be sure to mention it up front, because some days the captain may be running a morning and afternoon trip and the option will not be available.

It's a good idea to book your trip as far in advance as possible. Calling the night before and asking to fish the next day is not likely to book a top guide. They are often booked weeks and months in advance.

I do a little research before I book a guide. Friends and acquaintances are good sources for recommendations, but if none are available for my intended destination, I turn to the Internet. Most professional guides maintain Web sites that are easily found by Googling the particular location you want to fish. Organizations such as the Florida Guides Association (florida-guides.com) are also good sources for research. "These organizations," says Capt. Tom Van Horn, "hold their members to high standards. Members are required to prove their legitimacy annually." The Florida Guides Association requires its members to show annual proof of a Coast Guard captain's license, a state-issued vessel license that covers all the anglers on the boat, marine insurance (not required by the state) that includes liability coverage, and adherence to a stated code of ethics. The FGA's site and other sites like it provide e-mail and Web site addresses for anglers to visit and peruse. You can e-mail the captain and ask any particular questions you have about his offerings before you actually book.

Regularly posted fishing reports are another way to determine if your prospective guide will meet your needs. Many Florida master anglers post fishing reports on sites such as *Florida Sport Fishing* (floridasportfishing.com), *Sport Fishing* (sportfishingmag.com), *Cyber Angler* (cyberangler.com), *Florida Sportsman* (floridasports man.com), and a host of other reporting sites, as well as their own Web sites.

Trips Gone Bad—Expectations and Experiences

In order to get an idea of what guides expect of their clients, I asked them to describe their worst charter-fishing trip. These stories are the exception rather than the rule, but they are instructive in terms of identifying what your guide will expect of you on a charter. Names have been withheld to protect the innocent.

Several guides had stories about clients who tried to tell the guides how to fish or what to do. One said, "My hardest charters are when a client thinks they know everything—they usually don't, and it is hard for me to convince them otherwise." To make the most of a guided trip, go into it with an open mind and take advantage of the guides' expertise and local knowledge.

Another potential trip buster is alcohol. One guide described a trip that occurred during his first year of guiding. "My angler brought a bottle of whiskey and started to hit the bottle hard. Soon the whiskey took over and he was falling down drunk. I knew that he was a hazard to himself and also to me as his guide. I told him to please sit down, and I took off back to the dock, where I poured him off of the boat. I did not charge him for the day, I was just glad to be done with the matter."

Clients' expectations can also ruin a trip, as one guide revealed, "In my opinion, fishing shows on television depict catching fish as requiring no skill sets whatsoever. These same anglers would not attempt to run a marathon without proper training, but on their first time out fishing they want to set a world record."

In an effort to avoid disappointing a client with unrealistic expectations, most guides try to interview them when scheduling the charter. This is an effort to assure a match between the guide's expectations and the client's. "Generally speaking, I don't target fish species that are high on the degree of difficulty with a green angler on board, but especially not a green angler that has unreal expectations."

Another story about expectations points out the difference between fishing on a head boat and chartering a personal guide. In this story, a guide fished three anglers from out of town. They showed up at the dock with three empty coolers for the fish they were going to take back to their home town (1,000 miles away). "I explained that this was not that kind of trip and suggested that they go over to the beach and try to get on a head boat."

A story about a fly-fishing client drives home the point about expectations. On this particular trip, one of the guests—a fly angler—on the captain's boat boarded with a comment that no spinning equipment would be found on his boat back home. The fact is, the guest's fishing partner had requested the spinning equipment, and the captain had obliged. The "guest" stood on the bow for three hours with fly and fly rod in hand, line stripped on the deck, and never made the first cast to any of the fish that the captain pointed out to him. The guest claimed that he was a "sight fisherman" and he did not see any of the dozens of fish the captain pointed out to him. He berated the captain, telling him he didn't know what he was doing. This angler's delusion of self-grandeur ruined the trip for everyone. An honest evaluation of your own skills and expectations will go a long way toward having a successful charter.

This next story is cut short because the guide did not want to relive it, but the essential parts pretty much tell the tale. A client showed up for a trip with a big thermos of coffee and a bag of chocolate donuts. He proceeded to spill both and create a soggy mess. He also brought with him seven rods and reels, eighteen trays of tackle, and a forty-eight quart cooler full of live and dead bait, chum, sandwiches, and drinks. The guide mentioned to him that they didn't have that much room and that he would have to downsize considerably. The angler cut back to four rods and eight trays of tackle, but the cooler came on board. He insisted on using his prized baitcasters to continually cast into the wind, regardless of the fact that he fought bird nests all day long. As time passed, and the captain continued to reel in fish on his spinning reels and personal plugs, the angler finally decided to grab one of the captain's outfits and pull in some fish.

For many guides this story is like déjà vu all over again. The truth is, on any given day, it really does not take as many rods or as much tackle, food, drinks, or bait as many people think. Your guide can tell you all you need to know about what to bring on the trip. If you have any doubts, just ask.

Another story says a lot about expectations and planning your time with a guide. The trip looked great upfront—a two-day charter with a repeat client. But the client wanted to fish only on certain days and only at a particular time. He was told that the tide was going to be more favorable early in the day and again later. He said he didn't care, so the trip took place at the angler's selected time. The fish started to bite on the rising tide, but it was time to go because the angler had his own schedule to keep, and it had nothing to do with the guide's earlier prediction about when they should fish.

Although these experiences are rare, there are several things to learn from these stories. First, use your captain to help plan the trip in terms of days and time of the day to fish. When circumstances don't allow the perfect trip, go when you can, but don't be surprised when your expectations are not met. Secondly, be honest with the captain about your level of fishing experience and skill, so he can match your trip accordingly. Finally, take advantage of any possibility to fish two days in a row with the same captain—this will increase your odds of a successful trip. Believe me, captains are learning too. When one day turns out to be a bust, you can rest assured you are likely to see a different strategy the next day, so give him another chance.

Your Contributions to a Guided Fishing Trip

What to expect from your guide is only one side of the equation for a successful charter fishing trip. Your own behavior can be an important element in the success and enjoyment of the trip. With this in mind, consider a few selected comments from the guides when they were asked, "What do you expect from a client on a charter fishing trip?"

Guide #1. Guests should recognize that not every day will be full of fish and aim to share a fun day on the water.

Guide #2. I value clients who discuss their experience and level of fishing skills before the trip. I also like for them to let me know if inexperienced anglers, small children, or persons with special needs will be accompanying them on the trip. This information assists me in planning the strategy for the day.

Guide #3. Patience and willingness to listen is the best virtue of a prospective client. I want to accommodate them in every way. Their willingness to trust me and follow instructions will normally improve the day's productivity.

Guide #4. I really appreciate it when my clients show up on time and are prepared to deal with the weather and willing to listen and learn. I expect them to stay sober.

Guide #5. All I ask for in a client is that they are ready to enjoy their day on the water. That includes being willing to accept my judgments with respect to the fishing experience.

Guide #6. My charter service is catch-and-release only. I want them to do their research in advance and understand that we won't be keeping fish. I usually tell them this when they contact me.

Guide #7. I try not to have any preconceived expectations, because most people who book with me have indicated their fishing experience prior to booking. I just want them to be on time, courteous, prepared, and have a level of fishing experience that they previously described to me.

Guide #8. I'm always happy when clients arrive on time, have a positive attitude, and are open to instruction on how to fish the area. They should treat the guide's boat and equipment with care and respect and follow the guide's instructions.

Guide #9. I appreciate it when my clients give me a call if they are running late. They should bring personal items that they will need for the day—drinks, food, camera, jacket, and so on. They should dress like they are going fishing and not wear clothes that can't get dirty.

Guide #10. I ask my clients to wear boat-friendly shoes and schedule a fishing trip for best results by considering the position of the moon and the corresponding tides.

Guide #11. My expectations of the client depends on what they tell me prior to the trip. If they tell me what kind of equipment they are familiar with and what they consider their level of skill, I can plan their trip accordingly. I ask my clients to show respect for the rods, reels, tackle, boat, and other equipment they are provided as part of the charter.

Guide #12. I like my clients to be on time, not too early, not too late, about ten minutes before the scheduled time. Hopefully, they will listen carefully and implement the instructions that are given and ask questions if they don't understand. If they feel they had a rewarding, safe, productive trip, a reasonable tip is always appreciated.

What You Should Do When Hiring a Guide

Based on the observations above and on other comments from the guides, here is a checklist of do's and don'ts for hiring a guide. The list will provide you with some of the questions you can ask when you contact a prospective guide, plus it gives you some guidelines on how you can contribute to the success of the fishing trip.

1. Do Your Homework: The best way to ensure a quality fishing experience is to spend some time researching a guide's qualifications, background, experience, and knowledge. You can do this by calling, e-mailing, or checking them out on the Internet.

2. Book Early: Book your charter as soon as you know your available dates. Otherwise you may have to compromise and not get the date you want. Make your trip deposit on time, and mark your calendar to call the guide the day before to confirm. This confirmation relieves you and the guide of any worry about a no-show.

3. Verify Rates and Cancellation Policy: Be sure you know the price of the charter and any charges related to additional anglers, gas surcharges, live-bait charges, or other incidental costs. Also inquire about a cancellation policy.

4. Clarify Your Desires and Expectations: Let your chosen captain know what you would like to accomplish on the trip. Find out if lunch is provided or if you should bring your own. Let him know if you want to bring your own equipment, and identify any special needs.

5. Show Up on Time: Arrive on time with an open mind ready to follow your guide's instruction and advice. You hired him for his local knowledge, so take advantage of the opportunity to learn and increase your own knowledge base.

6. Respect Your Guide's Equipment: Professional guides pride themselves in the equipment they use. It is chosen for specific applications and is normally of the highest quality. The rod you will be using is not made for poking at crabs and other things or checking the depth of the water. Don't lay a rod on the deck where it can be stepped on and don't leave it where it can fall or be pulled overboard. Use this opportunity to learn about the equipment, why the guide chose it, and how he maintains it.

7. Comply with Your Guide's Policy on Alcohol: If you plan to bring alcohol with you, be sure to discuss it with your guide. Many guides do not allow any alcohol and some allow only beer and wine. Many

insurance policies will refuse a claim if alcohol has been consumed on the boat, because of the safety factor. Use common sense and remember you are going fishing, not drinking.

8. Tip Your Guide: Like any service business, it is traditional to tip your guide. An eight-hour charter is equivalent to a ten- to twelve-hour workday for the guide. He spends time before the trip traveling, preparing the boat, rigging tackle and equipment for the day. After your charter, he will spend more time cleaning the boat, preparing for the next day, and then traveling home. Base your tip on the standard 15-percent gratuity, but recognize when a guide goes beyond the call of duty to make your day an enjoyable one.

9. Be Careful: In case you don't know, rule number one on many charter boats is, "Don't Hook the Captain." Your guide should always be conscious of safety, and you should too. Be aware of your surroundings, and fish with respect toward everyone in the boat. Failure to fish safely can result in an unwanted accident and ruin the day for everyone.

Last Cast

Following the checklist above will make your next trip with a charter guide more pleasurable. However, beware the unscrupulous guide who wants nothing but your money. They are out there. Guides with no Coast Guard License, no vessel license, and no insurance are perfectly happy to take you on a boat ride for the price of your charter. More often than not, that price will be less than you will pay a reputable guide whose operating costs include proper licensing and insurance. You must do your homework before you choose your guide, and your choice should not be based solely on the lowest price. The small investment in time, made to thoroughly check out your guide, will pay big dividends and increase your opportunity for a fun and productive day on the water.

Captain Van Horn reminds us, "Fishing is fishing, and catching is catching; both are fun." Making a charter fishing trip fun and successful requires effort from both the guide, and the angler.

11

Environmental Realities

Guides' Perspectives on the State of the Resource

Recreational Trips by Mode of Fishing in Florida 2006

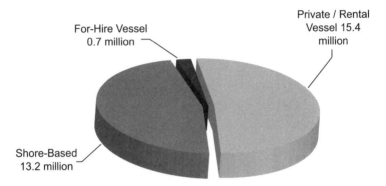

For-Hire Vessel
0.7 million

Private / Rental
Vessel 15.4
million

Shore-Based
13.2 million

Charter fishing makes up the smallest segment of the fishing population in Florida. Source: http://research.myfwc.com

Increased fishing pressure and habitat destruction are two of the most serious problems facing Florida's fishery resource today. Capt. "Bouncer" Smith says we have more people fishing with little knowledge of good conservation practices and the result is habitat destruction. He says, "A lack of conservation knowledge results in prop scars and buckets of dead baby fish. We need to see educational pieces on the evening news and local television magazines outlining the merits of good conservation practices." I have to agree. I have often wondered why I live in a county surrounded by water, but seldom do I see a news report related to fishing or conservation, unless it is a tragedy of some kind. I'm with Bouncer on this one; I would like to see some educational pieces on good conservation practices, so everyone who watches the evening news could be educated on the value of conservation.

Florida is consistently ranked as the most-visited fishing destination in the country. Because of this ranking, Florida proudly wears the banner of "Fishing Capital of the World." That's an effective marketing slogan and many businesses depend on the tourism created by our fisheries. Thousands of fishing visitors enjoy the spoils that

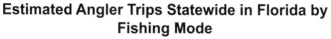

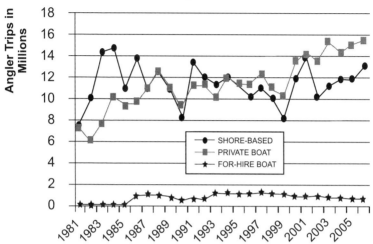

Fishing pressure in Florida continues to grow as more and more anglers visit the state to enjoy the abundant water resources. Source: http://research. myfwc.com

Florida has to offer, but increased fishing pressure and habitat destruction have long been taking their toll.

As seen by the chart on page 208, the 29.3 million fishing trips to Florida in 2006 were made up of 13.2 million shore-based anglers, 15.4 million private or rental-vessel anglers, and 0.7 million trips by guides on charter vessels. The graph above indicates a roller-coaster pattern of ups and downs since the early 1980s. However, the important point is that total fishing trips statewide have continually increased since 2002 to the current level of 29.3 million trips. There is no end in sight for this upward trend.

Given this increased fishing pressure, which in itself reduces the stock of fish available, it becomes extremely important that concerned anglers pay close attention to what is happening to the essential fish habitat that supports fishing in Florida. Defining habitat destruction is relatively simple. Habitat destruction is a change in land use where one habitat such as shoreline mangroves is replaced with another habitat such as residential or commercial development. The fish, plants, and other animals that previously inhabited the site are either displaced or, worse yet, destroyed.

Toxic runoff destroys fish habitat. Pesticides and other pollutants discharged into the waters kill seagrass meadows and replace them with barren bottom soil where no animals or plants can propagate.

Another example of habitat destruction is the damage caused by uncaring or careless anglers operating their vessels in water that is too shallow to navigate without damaging the underlying habitat. A visit to almost any shallow-water flat in Florida will reveal the damage done by motorboat props. Fragile grass beds are covered with prop scars that can take years to renew. With new scars added faster than old ones can heal, the outcome is very bleak.

Essential fish habitat includes both the water column and the underlying surface of our rivers, lakes, and oceans. According to the National Marine Fisheries Service, "Certain properties of the water column such as temperature, nutrients, or salinity are essential to various species. Some species may require certain bottom types such as sandy or rocky bottoms, vegetation such as seagrasses or kelp, or structurally complex coral or oyster reefs." Different fish species in Florida use different habitats as they move through a cycle of breeding, spawning, nursing, and simply hiding from their natural predators. Protecting fish habitats is absolutely necessary to ensure healthy vibrant fisheries now, as well as for our children.

A multiplier effect is at work for any successful protection and restoration of habitat. Much of Florida's ecosystem is edge habitat, where one type of environment blends with another. The same types of habitats that are critical for fisheries as spawning grounds, nurseries, fry rearing, food supply, and migration areas also provide essential habitat for many species of birds and other animals. That sounds like a win-win situation and would seem to provide a basis for cooperation between fishers, hunters, bird watchers, and other outdoor enthusiasts previously concerned only about their specific interests. There is strength in numbers, and a partnership of existing organizations could be extremely beneficial to habitat protection and use.

What Our Master Anglers Say

In order to obtain an angling point of view on existing and future environmental conditions, I asked the guides participating in the book to identify their two most pressing concerns, related to the health of the fishing resource in Florida. Their unique perspective is one of seeing the changes that occur on a daily basis, as well as those changes that have occurred over a period of time.

Habitat Destruction

The overwhelming concern of these master anglers is the issue of habitat destruction and the associated pollution brought on by over-development and population growth. Capt. Ron Tomlin summed it up in one sentence: "Over-population resulting in too much pressure, too little access, and too little water."

Captain Tomlin says we need to elect politicians who recognize the impact of development and growth when it is out of control, especially along Florida's coastlines. He says, "It would seem Florida may have reached its natural-resource limit, relative to the population of the state." Added pressure from visitors and developers only compounds the problem.

The state of Florida is growing fast, and it seems that everyone wants to live, work, and recreate on or near the coast. Capt. Pat Dineen says, "It's all about the number of people enjoying the resource. Habitat disruption and destruction from continued growth is a huge concern. Everywhere you look there is new development on the shore, increased traffic on the road, and more boats on the water." Captain Dineen observes seawalls and riprap replacing marsh grass and mangroves, while increased runoff and siltation reduce water quality and harm habitat. "I think the fundamental way to help preserve fisheries for the future is education regarding our own impacts on the water."

He compares, through personal observation, the environment of Florida with that of Hawaii. "Compared to Florida, Maui is spotless. A Hawaiian local coming here would be highly disturbed from all the litter and trash along the streets, in our parking lots and on the water. People over there simply do not litter." He describes Maui as physically beautiful with the mountains and the water, but what struck him the most was the lack of litter on the islands and how the people would go out of their way to pick something up and dispose of it. Attitudes and behavior may have to change for Florida to replace some of its lost beauty.

A connection between population increase and pollution is made by Capt. Ray Markham. "Increased population increases development pressure and adds to pollution. Destruction of habitat through pollution diminishes the ability of fish to grow in numbers and size." He suggests that a moratorium on urban growth and development, and more stringent restrictions on population density by government agencies would go a long way toward eliminating the destruction of critical habitat.

Capt. Tom Van Horn agrees, "I think the number one concern we should have as anglers is loss of habitat." As far as a solution, he says we need to convince other groups who have a similar stake in the outdoors and who think as we do to join us, and use the political system to bring about change. "I think the best solution is to convince lawmakers that recreational angling is more valuable than some condos along the shoreline. We convince them by expanding our circles of influence. The more people who utilize the resource, the more value it has."

Captain Van Horn's thinking combines economics and politics to seek a solution that will decrease habitat destruction, and the economics cannot be overlooked. We live in a capitalistic society where the bottom line often drives decisions. The coastal regions of Florida are a great economic engine that turns the wheels of commerce in many segments of the state's economy. Any decision to alter that engine must be weighed against the greater good of all the beneficiaries of Florida's fishery resource. Questions need to be asked and answered, such as this query from Captain Van Horn: "Is it better to build one more condo to benefit a few or save a shoreline to benefit many?"

It will likely take some strong partnerships to make progress toward protecting habitat. Capt. Chris Myers agrees. "Habitat destruction is an important issue, but one that anglers do not have much control over." He suggests joining organizations such as the Costal Conservation Association, commonly known as the CCA, the Florida Guides Association (FGA), or similar organizations to increase the political influence with legislators who might make a difference. Organizations such as these are proactive instead of reactive and have a much better chance of influencing decisions to protect and save our resource instead of having to rebuild it.

Another problem may be Florida's historic orientation toward management of a single species. Studies of snook, redfish, and sea trout are carried out to help manage those specific species. Although many anglers accept and support this single-species approach, an alternative is outlined by Capt. Keith Kalbfleisch. He believes it is time to turn management toward protecting specific habitats rather than particular fish. As an example he says, "We need to protect the flats habitat of the Indian River Lagoon, so more fish are maintained. Loss of habitat, such as grass flats, is the number one threat to our fisheries."

Capt. Rick Burns says, "Coastal development brings several things, including loss of habitat and water pollution from stormwater runoff carrying fertilizers, pesticides, and oil residue. The runoff results in nasty water, muck, algae growth, exotic weeds, and other forms of pollution." All these items have a deleterious affect on recreational fishing.

Captain Burns asks, "Why is the Mosquito Lagoon, Canaveral National Seashore, Keaton Beach in Taylor County, the Homosassa area, or even the coastal marsh area of Louisiana, to name a few, so good for fishing? I'll tell you why: No coastal development! And these areas have tons of fish taken out yearly and still keep producing good supplies of fish."

Future shoreline development should be subjected to new and innovative alternatives acceptable by all user groups. There are environmentally friendly alternatives to the old-fashion methods that subjected the shoreline to erosion and destruction. In some areas of the world, solid docks are being replaced by floating docks suspended over the shoreline, gentler slopes are used to connect the water with the shoreline, softer materials and natural vegetation are replacing steel and concrete sea walls, and development is being moved back from the shoreline to create buffer zones of natural vegetation between the water and the development.

Any notion of curbing development will be a hotly debated topic and far beyond the scope of this book to discuss in detail. Passions will run high on both sides of the issue and participants must approach it with an open mind and a goal of gaining the most good for the most people.

Protecting the habitat does seem to be the future of fishing in Florida, but more rules and regulations will also require more law enforcement.

Enforcement

The second most-common concern among the participating guides was the issue of enforcing existing laws that protect our fisheries. There are many laws on the books now that would go a long way toward protecting the resource if they could be enforced. We already read in chapter 9 how Florida Fish and Wildlife officers are responsible for enforcing the laws related to 208 species of freshwater fish and more than 500 species of saltwater fish. Add to this their other duties, and the fact that they are expected to assist Homeland Security as well as other law enforcement agencies, and the problem is abundantly clear. There simply are not enough wildlife officers, and there won't be enough in the future, if not planned for now. Not surprisingly, we are back to economics and politics.

Capt. Ray Markham observes, "There are not enough officers on the water to enforce regulations currently on the books. Only by the demands of citizens will politicians be directed to do what is necessary to ensure a healthy fishery. This includes raising more money through licensing." There are currently many exemptions from Florida's saltwater fishing license. For example, resident anglers fishing in saltwater from land or from a structure fixed to the land are not required to obtain a saltwater license. This is lost revenue that could be used for improving the resource. Captain Markham continues, "A saltwater license should be required for all anglers, with a few exceptions for age, disability, or other special conditions. These actions will raise money and secure matching government funds that will allow us to add proper enforcement."

The matching funds Captain Markham refers to come from the Federal Aid in Sport Fish Restoration Program. Details can be obtained on the Web at www.myfwc.com/fishing/Conservation/ Conserv_Progs_Federal_Aid.htm. Funds from the program are distributed based on a formula where small states get a minimum and larger states get a maximum allocation. The remaining states, a group which includes Florida, receive their share based on the size of the state and the number of licensed anglers. The key word in that statement is *licensed*. In Florida we have many exemptions to our license requirements, so seniors, youth, and resident shoreline anglers, who don't have to purchase a saltwater license to fish legally, don't count toward the allocation unless they voluntarily purchase a license.

Additionally, the program makes allocations based on *holders*, not number of licenses. This means an individual holding a saltwater license, a freshwater license, and a snook permit is counted only as one holder.

Organizations such as the FGA, CCA, and others are proponents of eliminating the shoreline exemption in order to add more paid recreational fishing licensed holders to Florida's statistics. Their efforts have not been successful and the shoreline exemption remains a part of Florida's licensing dilemmas.

With an already overburdened staff, FWC could use some help. One such helping-hand program currently exists in the Tampa area. Members of the FGA lend their eyes to fish and wildlife officers through the Trained Eyes Program. FGA members report resource violations to FWC, who take appropriate enforcement actions. Participating guides are trained by FWC to know what to look for and what to report. This pilot program is expected to be expanded to other portions of the state in the future.

This type of partnership sits well with Captain Van Horn. He agrees that more law enforcement is needed, but he doesn't try to shift the entire burden to FWC or other enforcement entities. He says, "We must look at ways to assist the state and federal agencies in enforcing existing rules." He suggests a voluntary program where guides could carry a law-enforcement officer in their boats, one day a year. Such a program would save the state the expense of a boat, fuel, and maintenance. "I know this idea would float like a lead balloon, but we are all going to have to be creative to save what we have left of our fishery."

If you don't think more enforcement is needed, just look around while you are fishing. You see the same uncaring anglers destroying our habitat, with fast boats and careless activities. I find myself asking, "Where are the marine officers when you need them?" The facts are, they can't be everywhere at once, and they can use our help. The anglers I know are creative in finding new ways to catch fish; I know they can think of creative ways to help save the habitat.

Other Conservation Issues

Several other conservation issues were brought up by the guides, including water quality, fish handling, catch and release, protected fishing areas, water access, and seagrass protection.

Water Quality

Although it is hard to separate the issue of water quality from all the other issues related to our fishing environment, it is worth mentioning independently. Whether from inadequately treated sewage treatment, agricultural runoff, or pesticide and fertilizer runoff from residential communities, the final result is reduced water quality. Florida's water was once clean and pure. Today much of it is green with nuisance algae blooms as polluted water is dumped or leached back to rivers, lakes, and nearshore waters. This unfavorable impact on the ecology and environment of our fishery must be reversed.

Captain Tomlin says, "We have allowed runoff from lawns, pastures, concrete, and asphalt to enter the water streams, destroying habitats and causing red-tide issues. We need to spend a lot of time and money to clean up the water and give it a chance to percolate back into the aquifer."

Strong agreement with this observation comes from Capt. Ed "Jazz" Jazwierski. He says, "I believe runoff and discharge would be one of my highest conservation concerns. The sugar and cattle industries have literally decimated the Everglades. It's still a beautiful place to go, but we're killing it." He also cites the runoff from cities after a heavy rain—oil, sludge, garbage, raw sewage, and fertilizer all seem to find their way into Tampa Bay, bringing the water quality down. "Habitat has been destroyed at an alarming rate for years. As homes and condos go up, pollution increases, and mangroves, which are the primary cover in the estuary, disappear. I say water quality and habitat destruction are a greater threat than gillnets because, if the habitat is destroyed, our fish can't survive."

To make his point on water quality, Captain Burns draws an analogy between fish and humans. "Fish, kind of like humans, have specific needs to exist and be satisfied. Fish need food, habitat, and water quality. Take away any of the three ingredients, and fish will go somewhere else to find the comfort and sustenance they need or they will cease to exist." As the food source is destroyed, the habitat depleted, and the water quality reduced, there are fewer and fewer places for the fish to go. "Florida is still the sport-fishing capital of the world, but if we fail to have enough people on the ground floor and in high places who care about our resource and want to keep it healthy, we will see it slowly and dramatically change for the worse."

Recognizing a problem is often said to be part of the solution, and in the case of water quality the solution will be expensive. Many do not like calling on government for help, but with this and other environmental issues, government is going to have to be part of the solution.

Fish Handling

With the regulations requiring the release of many fish because of size limits and closed seasons, handling of fish becomes an important conservation issue. Chapter 8 pointed out many ways that

A fish sling will keep a fish supported horizontally during hook removal and increase its chance of survival after release. Photo by Capt. Chris Myers.

anglers can handle and release fish so they have a good chance of surviving.

Capt. Chris Myers identifies one of his main conservation concerns as proper fish handling. He even uses a specially constructed cradle to land big redfish. Once caught and brought to the side of the boat, the fish is maneuvered into the sling and supported horizontally while he removes the hook. "My intent is to educate anglers on the proper care and handling of fish so that when the fish are released, they survive."

Most guides agree that proper fish handling should be addressed through education by fishery management officials, guides, and individual anglers, setting a good example for others to follow.

Catch and Release

Catch and release is another issue guides identified as important to conservation. Used as a method of conservation, this relates directly to the increased number of anglers in Florida. Imagine a school of 100 redfish being fished by only five guides. Imagine also that these five guides fished only three days a week with one client. This group could legally take fifteen redfish per week from this school of 100. You can do the math. How many weeks would it take to eliminate this massive school of 100 fish? If you got your calculator out, you came up with an answer of six-and-two-third weeks. Now, consider the actual number of working guides, add in the recreational anglers, and it should give you some idea of how quickly our fish stock can be depleted based on keeping only the legally allowable catch. Add poaching, illegal netting, and other non-legal forms of fish take, and the numbers become overwhelming.

Capt. John "GiddyUp" Bunch reports, "Recent studies have indicated a staggering revelation about snook. Sixty-three percent of all snook in Florida have been caught at least three times. In other words, because our fish are subjected to such abuse, we must take every action to eliminate the stress placed on our resource." Because of his keen interest in this issue, Captain GiddyUp promotes barbless circle hooks as a major tool of catch-and-release fishing.

In terms of trophy fish, today's technology related to fish replicas is a great reason for not killing the fish of a lifetime. A few measurements and a good photo will make it possible for you to have an exact duplication of the real thing, without killing the fish. This growing trend toward high-tech fish reproductions will leave more fish swimming and still provide a trophy for bragging rights.

Everyone knows that photographs are a great way to preserve fishing memories and conserve fish through catch and release. A great tip for all anglers is to know how everyone else's camera operates. Each angler should share the operating essentials of their own camera with others. Trying to figure out how to use a camera, while a fish is out of the water, is not a good conservation strategy. The longer fish are out of the water, the lower their chances of survival, so do everything in your power to get the fish you catch back in the water as soon as possible.

We all need to support catch and release as part of an overall strategy to protect our fishing resource now and in the future. If enough anglers practice catch and release, even part of the time, it could have a great positive impact on the fishery.

Protected Fishing Areas

Protected fishing areas are not always a popular topic among anglers, especially the ones that allow no fishing whatsoever. Nevertheless, areas such as "Pole and Troll" and "No-Motor Zones" have been used with great success in some areas of the state. The acceptance of such areas by guides and recreational anglers is likely to depend on just how severe the fishing restrictions are applied there.

Captain Van Horn says he could support more *green* angling areas. He runs his charters in the Indian River, Banana River, and Mosquito Lagoon and says he would support more no-motor zones, catch-and-release-only areas, pole-and-troll zones, and some short-term rotating Marine Protection Areas (MPA). The key word with respect to the MPAs is *rotating*. Most anglers naturally reject proposals that eliminate traditional uses of marine areas but would likely back limited closings, based on scientific data to support the need.

It may take some time to educate the public and gain their support for so-called green fishing areas, but if scientific data can be accumulated to show the benefits of these areas, more and more anglers will come on board.

Water Access

Access to boat slips and public ramps continues to dwindle. It is related directly to commercial development along our rivers and coasts. One horror story occurred here, in my neck of the woods, after a hurricane destroyed a local marina. That damage was bad, but worse yet was the fact that the marina would be lost to general public access forever. The marina was bought by a developer for construction of a condo and associated high-dollar slips. This is just one example of many across Florida, where slips were once rented for $10 to $12 a foot but now are sold for as much as $200,000 or more. The average angler and boater are left out of this equation.

Recreational anglers, who once had access to a variety of public facilities. now wait in long lines before launching for a day of fishing at the few public ramps that are still available. Capt. Merrily Dunn says she is very concerned with the limited access available to boaters and fishers. "My concern is that we are being limited in our access to the public waterways, and it's not just at boat ramps. Just about any region in the state has shorelines complete with houses from county line to county line."

Public and private boat ramps are dwindling each year. Captain Dunn cites the increasing expense to keep marinas running as the main reason there are more condos and less access for the public. "I don't know the right answer, but it is not cutting the people out of their right to have access to our public waters."

There is a growing contingency of anglers who feel the same way as Captain Dunn. Florida needs to maintain, and finally increase, public access to the waterways. Some means need to be found to slow shoreline development that gobbles up public-access points. Captain Dunn sees the solution as stopping big developers from buying out what is left of our shorelines, especially mangrove, marsh, or sandy beaches. Capt. Ron Tomlin tunes in by saying, "We cannot afford to see the continuing demise of the access points to the coastlines and lakes of the state because of development."

Seagrass Protection

Either human error or stupidity is the cause of much of the loss to our precious seagrass meadows. The easiest way to protect them is by preventing damage in the first place.

"There is currently too much angling pressure on our resource," says Captain Van Horn. "So changes must be made to keep it sustainable. Not only do we have to change the rules and regulations, but also our own attitudes. Running shallow must stop. This practice is bad for our inshore fishery, and we can only change it by changing our attitudes."

Seagrass protection is one area where we, as individual anglers, can do something about the problem, and many of us can start in our own backyard. It doesn't matter, if you live on the shore of a river, in an inland subdivision, or along the coastal waters of the state, use caution and good judgment when applying fertilizers and pesticides to your property. Runoff from these chemicals will impact the seagrasses in a harmful way.

We can also use maps, when boating, to learn where the channels are and to avoid areas too shallow to navigate. Running aground in the seagrass will produce prop scars that take years to recover. Wearing polarized sunglasses will help you see the shallow areas in time to avoid them. If you are in doubt about the depth of an area, slow down and idle. Be prepared to raise your engine, or stop it if needed.

Last Cast

Sometimes it is easier to identify and write about the problems than it is to solve them. Nonetheless, recognizing that we have problems with our fishery brings us a little closer to solving some of them and hopefully limiting the damage that we as humans are often the source of.

We must respect and protect our resources or we won't have any fish or fishing spots left for our grandchildren and their children. Captain Burns agrees, and says, "If you don't believe that, you haven't lived and fished here all your life. There are fewer fish and fewer habitats, compared to only twenty years ago."

Human actions are the biggest threat to the fishery resource—but also the best hope to protect it. We need to work together in partnerships, using scientific research to provide the data, on which we humans base our decisions regarding the management and protection of Florida's precious fishery resource. In 2006 more than two million saltwater anglers contributed $3 billion in retail sales, with more than 180 million fish landed. This statistic, according to the Florida Oceans and Coastal Council, makes Florida the number-one fishing state in the United States. Personally, I intend to look at my time and money spent in the name of conservation as an investment in the future of our great sport of fishing.

12

Final Secrets

Don't Tell

The passion for fishing demonstrated by Florida's master anglers is something to behold. Their every waking moment is dedicated to fishing and finding better ways to fish. This chapter will introduce you to the guides who participated in this book and will reveal their final secret for successful fishing.

After providing their fishing tips and philosophies in the book, they were asked to identify their greatest secret to successful fishing.

Responses to the question are included in their biographies below. You may be surprised to find that many are not so much secrets related to physical techniques, as they are common sense and mental conditioning.

Capt. John "GiddyUp" Bunch

He does his fishing somewhere between ten inches from the shoreline to ten miles offshore in the Pine Island Sound area of southwestern Florida. The coastal environment is natural to John—he grew up on a small barrier island off the coast of Charleston, South Carolina. John served five years in the United States Marine Corps after which he did a stint with IBM. After IBM, he gained his credentials to be a professional golfer. It was on a fishing trip with some of his golf buddies that he caught his first tarpon, an event that caused him to change his life forever. He made what he calls "the perfect decision." He gave up his golf career to pursue a career in fishing.

John specializes in tarpon but is also well known for trolling nearshore and inshore for grouper. He is a frequent speaker, writer, and radio personality in southwestern Florida. He regularly gives fishing seminars at *Florida Sportsman* Fishing and Boat shows. John is the founder and creator of Operation Open Arms, an organization dedicated to providing homeland support for our troops who are on leave from foreign-duty stations, including free fishing trips, lodging, meals, and other services.

Captain GiddyUp's Final Secret

The secret to successful fishing is two-fold. First, prepare the night before and have a plan. Execute the plan, and if it doesn't pan out have a backup plan already devised. Second, slow down. Don't run fifty miles per hour from one location to another, travel at twenty-five miles per hour and keep your eyes on the water. You'll see twice as much as you read the water, instead of just trying to get to your next location. Fishing success involves preparation, planning, and the ability to observe at the highest level.

Contact Information

GiddyUp Fishing Charters
Telephone: 239-283-8838
Cell phone: 239-822-8888
E-mail: jbunchie@aol.com
Web sites: www.captgiddyup.com; www.operationopenarms.com

Capt. Rick Burns

Capt. Rick Burns is a third-generation native of Florida, with more than thirty years' experience on the waters of west-central Florida near Homosassa. As a boy, his father introduced him and his three brothers to hunting and fishing all over Florida.

Florida's Nature Coast provided the perfect opportunity for Rick to engage in charter fishing. He fished tournaments for a while before turning his interest to charter fishing. Taking other people fishing and getting paid for it allowed Rick to begin his career doing what he loved to do. His enjoyment for guiding comes from his pure love of the challenges presented by angling and for the opportunity to teach fishing techniques to others. Captain Burns specializes in putting clients on redfish, tarpon, shallow-water grouper, spotted sea trout, and yes, even bluegill, using fly, spinning, and plug-casting equipment.

He serves on the pro staff of numerous tackle manufacturers and writes weekly and monthly articles for various outdoor publications.

Proving that fishing runs deep in this family, Rick and his wife, Bonnie, founded the Floral City Anglers. They oversee more than 100 members in their positions as president and vice president.

Captain Burns's Final Secret

Captain Burns says fishing success is closely related to having an open mind. Every day on the water is different and anglers must adapt to the changing conditions. Don't get hung up on a single lure or single natural bait. Experiment when the fish aren't biting—try different baits, different colors, and different locations. Flexibility just may become your secret to success.

Contact Information

Reel Burns Charters
Telephone: 352-726-9283
Cell phone: 352-302-5524
E-mail: reelburns2001@yahoo.com
Web site: www.reelburns.com

Capt. Pat Dineen

This Emerald Coast captain's job may find him in six inches of water one day and 600 feet the next. Captain Dineen's fishing charters range from Navarre Beach to Panama City. He and his wife, Toni, have been married for ten years, and his daughter, Katie Anne, carries the same name you will see on the side of his Pathfinder.

Captain Dineen was led to charter fishing after holding an office job as an environmental consultant. Given his lifetime love for fishing and his accumulated knowledge and experience, he decided to exchange his business office for one with a "panoramic view."

His specialty is catching fish and making sure his clients have fun doing it. He caters to sport- and fly-fishing enthusiasts and guides sight-fishing anglers for redfish in the winter, cobia in the spring, and tarpon during June and July. He also captains for the Campbell Fishing Team, fishing throughout the Bahamian Islands during winter months.

On the Sunsport Network's award-winning *Chevy Florida Fishing Report*, Captain Dineen is the regional expert for Florida's Panhandle area, and he has been featured on numerous other television programs. He is a contributing writer for *Florida Fishing Weekly* and a member of the Florida Outdoor Writers Association.

Captain Dineen's Final Secret

If you want to catch more fish, you have to fish where the fish are. Time and experience will tell you that. Then, be patient and use good techniques. Captain Dineen says to minimize your terminal tackle if you want to get more bites and put more fish in the boat.

Contact Information

Flyliner Charters, Inc.
Telephone: 850-376-0400
E-mail: flyliner@cox.net
Web site: www.flyliner.com

Capt. Merrily Dunn

There are more than 1,100 Orvis-Endorsed Fly-Fishing Guides—only about fifty are women. One of those fifty is Capt. Merrily Dunn.

Living near the water in Sarasota was a positive element in her decision to become a fishing guide. She managed a one-hour photo lab as an occupation but was always thinking about fishing.

She does most of her guiding on Florida's Suncoast in the Sarasota area, with a specialty in light-tackle or fly-fishing for inshore species.

Her success as a professional guide led her to tournament fishing, and she's had many impressive finishes. She was ranked among the top twenty-five redfish teams in the country in 2003, and she is the first woman angler to fish an Oh Boy! Oberto Redfish Cup top five, finishing in fourth place in Chalmette, Louisiana, in 2005. She is a big promoter of catch-and-release and environmentally friendly fishing.

Captain Merrily's Final Secret

Never think that you've learned it all. Keep your mind open to using different fishing methods and learn from others who have been successful. Anglers are only human and can't make the fish bite, but because they have the capacity to learn they can be prepared when the fish do decide to eat. Merrily lives by the age-old maxim of a Roman philosopher who said, "Luck is what happens when preparation meets opportunity."

Contact Information

Coastal Fishing Adventures, Inc.
Telephone: 941-750-8135
Cell phone: 941-812-3474
E-mail: ReelSaltyLady@msn.com
Web site: www.coastalfishingadventures.com

Capt. Dale Fields

Capt. Dale Fields grew up fishing the banks of the Hillsborough River in North Tampa. The biggest influences on his early fishing years were his dad and his uncle, who both fished all of Tampa Bay and areas northward. With such role models, he couldn't help but catch the fishing bug.

Dale was a firefighter for many years, and his work schedule provided plenty of time to continue his fishing pursuits. During these years, he fished with a good friend who one day made the suggestion that, given Dale's skills and experience, he should become a charter captain. The idea stuck and Dale began his charter-fishing career.

Captain Fields specializes in inshore and nearshore fishing for all saltwater varieties. His fishing area ranges from the mouth of Tampa Bay near St. Petersburg northward along the Gulf Coast and Intracoastal Waterway to New Port Richey.

Captain Fields's Final Secret

Captain Fields's final fishing secret relates to the tides. If you want to improve your fishing success, fish in moving water. Plan your trip during good strong tides and your probability of success will soar. He also suggests that anglers not take fishing too seriously. For him, fishing is a way to enjoy what nature has to offer. All you have to do is be out there to enjoy the sunrise and the sunset.

Contact Information

Flats Meow Charters
Telephone: 813-973-2311
Cell phone: 813-917-7906
E-mail: flatsmeow7222@verizon.net
Web sites: www.flatsmeowfishing.com; www.floridafishing.com/
guides/fields

Capt. Rick Grassett

Nothing succeeds like success. For this Delaware native, Florida—
specifically, the areas around Sarasota Bay, lower Tampa Bay, and
Gasparilla Sound in Charlotte Harbor—turned out to be the perfect
place to find it.

Rick grew up hunting and fishing on the Chesapeake Bay and the
rivers and ponds of the Delmarva Peninsula but moved to Florida in
1981. He and his wife Karen have two grown kids and two grandchildren. Rick had long harbored a dream to become a professional fishing guide. He started guiding part-time to support his fishing habit
and, in the process, developed a niche for himself in the industry. He
quickly became so busy he made his guiding a full-time vocation.

Rick fishes the bays, backcountry, and coastal Gulf waters from
Tampa Bay to Charlotte Harbor. His specialties are fishing with flies
and artificial lures. He is an Orvis-Endorsed Fly-Fishing Guide. In
addition to his Sun Coast area charters, Captain Grassett has lead
groups of fly anglers to remote fishing locations around the world.

Rick is also an accomplished outdoor writer. He serves as a field
editor for *Saltwater Angler* magazine and writes for several more
outdoor publications. He also stays active on the conservation
front.

Captain Grassett's Final Secret

There is no need to memorize fishing spots. Instead, learn when
and how to fish certain characteristics. Try to learn why the fish
are there, as opposed to making an inventory of spots to fish. If you

learn why fish congregate at certain locations, you can find other spots with the same characteristics. Follow this simple advice and you will be successful.

Contact Information

Snook Fin-Addict Guide Service, Inc.
Telephone: 941-923-7799
E-mail: snookfin@aol.com
Web sites: www.snookfin-addict.com; www.flyfishingflorida.net

Capt. Richard Grathwohl

Growing up on his father's and grandfather's charter boats out of Wood Cliff Canal in Freeport Long Island instilled the love of fishing in Captain Grathwohl's blood. His move to Florida drove the passion even deeper. Living in Marathon, Captain Grathwohl traveled to school in a skiff and after school went diving, swimming, tending lobster traps, or fishing in what he called a wonderland for a seventh grader. What other destiny could there be but that of a charter captain?

Captain Grathwohl now follows his passion in the Florida Keys where the Gulf of Mexico meets the Atlantic. He specializes in flats fishing for bonefish, tarpon, permit, mangrove snapper, barracuda, and sharks. This third-generation charter captain continues a long family tradition as he enters his thirty-sixth year of charter fishing, with an unbelievable accumulation of knowledge related to fishing and the resource. He puts his knowledge and experience to use by participating in conservation meetings around the state.

Captain Grathwohl's Final Secret

The secret to successful sight-fishing is definitely in the eyes. Never neglect the importance of training your eyes to improve your fishing. You can train them when you are driving down the road or sitting in your backyard. Scan the area beyond your immediate position and then back toward you. Look for and note mentally anything out of the ordinary. Train your eyes to focus and pick up on any anomaly in the water around you.

Your casting might be great, but if you can't pick out a fish or a school of fish when called out at three o'clock, forty feet, the best casting skills in the world will do no good. You have to be prepared to spot the fish and make the cast. If you have to ask, "Where are they now?" it is likely to be too late.

Contact Information

Fish 'N Fever
Telephone: 305-743-5122
Cell phone: What's that?
E-mail: rfishnfever@bellsouth.net

Capt. Danny Guarino

Captain Guarino was born in Tampa, Florida, in 1954 and has lived and fished the West Coast of Florida all his life. He spent twenty-five productive years in the banking industry, rising to the position of vice president before making a decision to leave his coat-and-tie job as a banker for the guide shirt and shorts of a professional fishing guide.

Dan's specialty is snook, but he also guides his clients to impressive catches of redfish, trout, and tarpon in the shallow waters of the Tampa Bay flats. He is a conservation-minded angler, staying active in various environmental issues related to the future of fishing.

Captain Guarino's Final Secret

Dan's secret to successful fishing is summed up in a word: persistence. Persistence is a characteristic that anglers either have or they don't. If they don't have it they should develop it. Frank Lloyd Wright once said, "I know the price of success: dedication, hard work, and an unremitting devotion to the things you want to see happen." Persistence in fishing is like that; you don't have to catch fish every time, but you do need to give your best effort to be successful at it.

Contact Information

D. R. Guarino Charters
Cell phone: 813-956-2010
E-mail: ShPoint@aol.com
Web site: www.fishingguidetampabay.com

Capt. Ed "Jazz" Jazwierski

Riding his bike to go fishing in a lake or creek was a normal childhood activity for this city boy growing up in Chicago. His passion for fishing was so strong that he would drive miles to feed his fishing habit. During one four- or five-year period, while chasing smallmouth bass, walleye, musky, and steelhead, he actually held year-round fishing licenses in Illinois, Indiana, Wisconsin, Michigan, and Ohio.

He was introduced to Florida fishing when his parents bought a second home in Tampa. He would visit them with one goal in mind—going fishing every day. He began to look forward to his visits but dreaded going home. The constant presence of snook and tarpon dancing in his head was just too much; he was hooked on light-tackle saltwater sport fishing. With the support of family and friends, he moved to Tampa Bay to start a new page in his life.

Even while living in Illinois, he had people telling him he should become a fishing guide, because he enjoyed taking people fishing. When he moved to Florida he made that idle suggestion become a reality. He earned his Coast Guard license and began his charter business fishing in the salt that he came to love. Given his supportive wife, Jill, and a realization that fishing will not make him a millionaire, he is content to do what he loves best.

Captain Jazz's Final Secret

If you want to improve your fishing success, learn to adapt to your surroundings and conditions. Think like a fish. If it's winter with low water temperatures, fish areas that are out of the wind; fish south-facing structure, where the water has been exposed longer to the warming of the sun. Even a two-degree rise in water temperature can improve the bite. In the summer when the water temperatures are high, start early and work the mangroves or other shorelines that are facing west. These areas will be shaded from the sun and remain cooler longer.

If you're not catching fish like you want, don't be afraid to try new places and new techniques. Be open-minded and creative in your approach to fishing. Don't cheat yourself, or you'll never know what you could be catching. Think smart and fish hard.

Contact Information

Fishin' Tampa Bay
Telephone: 727-409-6733
E-mail: info@fishintampabay.com
Web site: www.fishintampabay.com

Capt. Keith Kalbfleisch

Captain Kalbfleisch has been fishing in Florida for more than thirty years—the past fifteen have been concentrated on the East Coast of central Florida near Orlando. He grew up in Idaho, Thailand, and Florida. He has fishing experience from around the world, ranging from blue marlin in deep water to redfish on the flats.

His specialties include inshore and nearshore fishing. He is equally at home providing anglers the challenge of a trophy fish on a fly as he is at putting inexperienced anglers on the catch of a lifetime. His passion for fishing is witnessed by the joy he receives from taking other anglers fishing.

Captain Kalbfleisch is well known in the East Coast area of Florida and is often doing seminars at area venues. He has been featured on local television and radio shows, as well as in major fishing publications.

Captain Kalbfleisch's Final Secret

Success is in the details. Successful fishing takes more than a rod, reel, and bait. It requires paying attention to what is going on around you. The list of questions you can answer by simply observing your surroundings is endless.

Start by observing successful local anglers. What lure do they use? How fast are they working it? How far are they casting? What size line are they using? How heavy is the leader? What kind of cover or structure are they fishing? Don't take a broad-brush approach; get down to details and then try to duplicate what you have learned through observation.

If you are fishing shallow water, notice the behavior of the birds, watch for bait schools, start noticing how different kinds of fish make different kinds of wakes, pay attention to the bottom contours, keep your eyes and ears peeled for anything out of the ordinary. No detail is too small to note.

Contact Information

Saltwater Adventures of Central Florida
Cell phone: 321-279-1344
E-mail: capt-keith@saocf.com
Web site: www.capt-keith.com

Capt. Ray Markham

Growing up on the Suncoast in Pinellas County and fishing the in-shore and offshore waters and rivers of Florida's West Coast, Capt. Ray Markham was a natural to become a professional fishing guide. While growing up, his father and grandfather had cabins on the Withlacoochee and Chassahowitzka Rivers. Ray cut his teeth on bass and bluegill with spin, plug, and fly gear using artificial baits. With the exception of the size and species of the fish, spin, plug, and fly tackle remain his specialty today.

In his early career as a field tester for lure and tackle manufacturers, Captain Markham was often asked to take the firms' customers fishing. He gained notoriety through his outdoor writing and more requests to go fishing resulted. He decided to get his captain's license, first as a matter of education, but the continuing requests for fishing trips led him to start his charter business.

Along his long path of fishing adventures, Ray became the co-host of *Florida Sportsman Magazine Radio Live* out of Tampa and the west-central field editor for *Florida Sportsman*, and he currently writes a fishing column for the *Tampa Tribune* called "On the Waterfront." Captain Markham is also a seminar speaker at *Florida Sportsman* Fishing shows around the state.

Captain Markham's Final Secret

There aren't really any secrets to fishing, just information that you keep to yourself. However, knowledge is one of the few things you can share but never give away, you will always have it. There is no substitute for time on the water, and that time will help you gain knowledge of the habitat, the tides, the fish, and all the other relevant information you need to be successful. The more knowledge you have, the more productive you will be as an angler.

Captain Markham adds, don't forget to practice. All the knowledge in the world won't do you much good, if you can't make accurate casts at needed distances. It's an old cliché that practice makes perfect, and it doesn't apply anywhere more than in fishing.

Contact Information

Ray E. Markham
Telephone: 941-723-2655
Cell phone: 941-228-3474
E-mail: flatback@tampabay.rr.com

Capt. Robert McCue

This former United States marine is a conservationist at heart. Capt. Robert McCue has established himself as a well-known west-central and southwestern Florida guide while championing many high-profile conservation-related fishery issues, including attaining game-fish status for redfish in Florida and the passing of the Net Limitation Amendment that helped protect saltwater fish from unnecessary killing, overfishing, and waste.

Captain McCue is called upon by world-renowned fishery biologists to assist in tagging and sampling programs for several species of fish statewide. In 2005, 2006, and 2007, he led the state in providing fin clippings to tarpon researchers for DNA samples.

Rob's love for fishing and the resource has been with him since early childhood. He would hang around charter boats at the marinas and sometimes work for the captains. Now, and for the last twenty years, he is leading his clients to numerous world records and tournament victories. His specialties are inshore, nearshore, flats, and backcountry fishing.

Captain McCue is well known for his belief that the resource should be protected and available for all to enjoy. On the home front, he lives a quiet private life surrounded by his family. His greatest ambition is to see his daughter, Sara, graduate from college.

Captain McCue's Final Secret

Ninety percent of fishing is about finding your prey. By keeping your eyes and ears open, fish will often reveal their location through signs to an observant angler. The signs may be the sound of a school of bait being flushed along a bank, an unusual push or swirl of water, a flash, or a shadow contrasting against the bottom. By recognizing signs within your surroundings and integrating them with times of the year, water temperatures, tidal flows, and other pertinent details, a savvy angler will begin to formulate patterns.

While some anglers will record the factors surrounding a successful day in writing, the best fishermen also store this information in their memory and recall it when they witness or hunt for the same pattern again. The best anglers have no real secrets but have developed a keen sense about everything around them and remember how to capitalize on their experience.

Contact Information

Bounty Hunter Sport Fishing Guide Service, Inc.
Telephone: 1-800-833-0489
E-mail: Robert@gianttarpon.com
Web site: www.GiantTarpon.com

Capt. Troy Mell

This captain's love for fishing started a long way from Florida. Capt. Troy Mell grew up in Reading, Pennsylvania, where he spent every available weekend traveling to the Maryland coast to fish. He gained charter-boat experience while working on his father's charter boat and stayed connected to the industry while working in hotel management in various resort and fishing locations.

Cold northern weather and the attraction of Florida's clear waters enticed Captain Mell to move to Florida. His love for the water, his fishing experience, and the enjoyment gained from meeting and fishing with new people led him to start his professional fishing career. When not fishing professional redfish tournaments, Captain Mell guides out of Islamorada, Florida. His specialty is tarpon and redfish.

Troy has fished twenty-three professional redfish tournaments with one win, seven top-ten, and six top-twenty finishes to his credit. When not busy fishing, Captain Mell enjoys giving fishing seminars at various outdoor events.

Captain Mell's Final Secret

Even the name of his charter business contains a subliminal hint to his secret to success. This play on words, "Reel Mell-O Charters," suggests a mellowed-out captain who looks at fishing as a way to loosen up and have some fun. His advice is to relax, have fun, and enjoy your fishing; the catching won't be far behind.

Contact Information

Reel Mell-O Charters
Telephone: 305-393-0232
E-mail: reelmello@bellsouth.net
Web site: www.reelmello.com

Capt. Chris Myers

Sight-fishing with light and fly tackle in east-central Florida is the passion of this dedicated angler. Capt. Chris Myers grew up in South Florida before moving to the Orlando area some twenty years ago. He began fishing the shallow waters of the Indian River and Mosquito Lagoon because they were the closest saltwater fishing to his home. Week in and week out, he dedicated his fishing pursuits to learning his home waters like the back of his hand.

Once he became familiar with the water and confident in his ability to find fish, he started his charter business. He specializes in shallow-water sightfishing for redfish, trout, drum, and tarpon, using light tackle and fly equipment. He describes guiding as fishing through the eyes of another angler, with a daily challenge to make your angler's day the best he has ever experienced. Besides that, he says, there is no better office anywhere than the one he occupies every day on the water.

Captain Myers's Final Secret

Captain Myers identifies the secret to successful fishing as paying attention to details. He says little things make a difference and the more attention you give to them the better angler you will be. In his mind, fishing success comes with dedication, practice, and hard work, and that is the responsibility of each individual angler.

Contact Information

Central Florida Sight Fishing Charters
Telephone: 321-229-2848
E-mail: info@floridafishinglessons.com
Web site: www.floridafishinglessons.com

Capt. Jim Savaglio

As a kid on Long Island, Jim loved the outdoors, including fishing, clamming, and surfing the beaches in the New England summer. Captain Savaglio had early aspirations to be a wildlife biologist, but economic realities suggested a different path.

Switching careers from wildlife biologist to chemical manufacturing led him to work for several major pharmaceutical and medical-device manufacturers. During this time, offshore manufacturing was booming, and his job took him overseas to some beautiful and interesting places. China, Mexico and Europe were attractive, but returning home and hearing the immigration personnel say, "Welcome home," was always most comforting to him.

The rigors of traveling, being away from his wife, and old-fashion homesickness always went away after spending a few days fishing, hunting, and enjoying his family. During this time, his dream to become a captain and make his hobby a career would surface.

When not tournament fishing or running charters, Captain Savaglio shares his passion for the outdoors, his fishing knowledge, and his expertise in seminars, writing, and on radio shows. He works with a constant eye toward advancing and promoting the sport of fishing and conservation issues.

Captain Savaglio's Final Secret

Captain Savaglio's final offering sounds like it might come from a management book. Plan, practice, and execute, and success will follow. Plan each trip using the available knowledge in your arsenal. Practice your skills until they are routine. Execute from a basis of confidence, and finally, use every day as a learning experience for the fishing trips that will come in the future.

Contact Information

Inshore Slam Fishing
Telephone: 941-238-7597
E-mail: captain@inshoreslam.com
Web site: www.inshoreslam.com

Capt. "Bouncer" Smith

Three hundred sixty-five days a year, 400 trips a year; you do the math. You read that right; Capt. "Bouncer" Smith logs nearly 400 trips a year by running his thirty-three-foot Dusky out of Miami Beach Marina, on both day and evening trips. His numerous trips find him and his clients in search of beach tarpon and inlet snook in the nearshore waters; sailfish, kings, tuna, snapper and grouper along the edge of the Gulf Stream; and deep-water swordfish and dolphin twenty miles offshore.

Bouncer was born in Michigan and moved to Miami in 1956 at the tender age of seven. By the age of eight, he had caught his first sailfish and the saga began. Surrounded by great fishing buddies, clients, and family, Bouncer became one of the best-known guides along the Gold Coast of Florida.

Using the *Miami Herald Fishing Guide* to steer the way, he piled up numerous personal and client-held fishing records. Bouncer himself caught the fly-rod record for Pacific halibut, at 111 pounds on 20-pound tippet. Anglers on his boat have held more than fifty world records. This kind of success does not come by luck. For this captain it came as the result of his total addiction to fishing, from five years of age to present.

Captain Bouncer has spent his spare time, if you can imagine he had any, fishing with Make-a-Wish kids, doing a couple of seminars a month and making weekly call-in fishing reports. He did a radio fishing report for twenty-four years, did a TV fishing report one year, and has appeared on sixteen nationally aired fishing shows. He has also been the recipient of numerous conservation awards for his efforts toward protecting the fishing resource.

Captain Bouncer's Final Secret

Bouncer's secret mirrors his life. He has been successful, and you will too if you follow his simple advice. Share your love of fishing with everyone you can.

Contact Information

Bouncer's Dusky 33
Telephone: 305-573-8224
Cell phone: 305-439-2475
E-mail: captbouncer@bellsouth.net
Web site: www.captbouncer.com

Capt. Dave Sutton

This transplanted captain from Rhode Island started his guiding career in Pulaski, New York, on the Salmon River fishing for big browns, rainbows, and king salmon. Captain Sutton once held a New York State record for rainbow trout at 16 pounds, 8 ounces. In 1988 he relocated to South Florida where he now guides in the Fishing Capital of the World.

Captain Sutton spends more than 280 days a year chasing his specialty: bonefish. He also guides anglers in pursuit of permit, tarpon, snook, redfish, and spotted sea trout with artificial lures. Nicknamed the "Bone Crusher," he fishes his share of tournaments and has a few trophies to show for his effort. His anglers have most of the trophies, and he says that's the way it should be.

Although he prefers the salt and catch-and-release fishing, he is sometimes spotted in fresh water chasing Florida bass and peacock bass. He lives in the Redlands, just west of Homestead, Florida, with his marine-artist wife, Julie. He says this is the perfect location for a guide to live, because he is minutes from Biscayne Bay and the entrances to the Keys and the Everglades.

Dave is an established outdoor writer and columnist for many regional sportfishing publications and has appeared on numerous television shows.

Captain Sutton's Final Secret

Captain Sutton says you can't get enough of it, patience that is. Almost everything you do related to fishing requires patience. Patience is spending time to learn the area you fish. Patience is learning the habits of your prey. Patience is learning the weather patterns. Patience is not being too hasty in moving on to the next spot, if you think you are in the right spot to begin with. Patience is waiting until the tide is just right. Patience is one of the most valuable virtues in life; practice it in your fishing and perfect it in your life.

Contact Information

On the Flats Charters
Telephone: 305-248-6126
Cell phone: 786-564-6347
E-mail: djsutton@bellsouth.net
Web sites: www.saltwater-flyfisherman.com; www.OnTheFlats Charters.com.

Capt. Ron Tomlin

Capt. Ron Tomlin was born in Lake Wales, Florida, on a ranch adjoining the Kissimmee River. After losing his dad in 1958, he began a lifetime of fishing with his uncle who helped him develop a devoted love for fishing the Everglades. He moved to Lakeland in 1959, but the 'Glades were in his heart and his passion for fishing continued there throughout the years.

When the opportunity arose, he established his fishing-charter operation, mostly in the Everglades National Park and Ten Thousand Islands areas. His charters often entail multi-day fishing and camping trips in the remote Everglades backcountry. His real passion is showing other anglers how to chase snook in the Everglades using artificial lures.

Captain Tomlin's Final Secret

Captain Tomlin doesn't miss a beat when he says the most important secret of successful fishing is patience. He describes patience as understanding that when you are throwing artificial bait, in an area like the Everglades National Park, you may make many casts before you find fish willing to hit your lure. You will need to understand that the fishing at a slack tide is sometimes slow, and you may have to wait until the water starts moving again for the fish to get active. And patience is required for more than just catching fish. You'll need to learn not to jerk a lure that you just tossed into the mangroves, but instead counting to three before you gently try to dislodge it with finesse. It's also learning to slow down and enjoy every moment of your fishing experience.

Contact Information

Natural High Adventures
Telephone: 863-660-5428
E-mail: rtomlin@tampabay.rr.com
Web site: www.naturalhighadventures.net

Capt. Tom Van Horn

Capt. Tom Van Horn is a native Floridian with more than forty years of experience fishing Florida's waters. He grew up in central Florida and currently guides in the North Indian River, Banana River, and the Mosquito Lagoon, as well as the nearshore waters of Ponce De Leon and Port Canaveral inlets. He has served as a firefighter at the Kennedy Space Center for twenty-seven years. His specialty is light-tackle fishing and fly fishing from paddle craft in the Banana River No-Motor Zone.

A real outdoor enthusiast who likes to get involved, Captain Tom is serving the Anglers for Conservation organization as its first president. He writes regular columns in several outdoor publications.

Captain Van Horn's decision to become a charter captain was an easy one, since he has always loved taking other people fishing. His entry into the charter-fishing industry turned his dreams into reality, by giving him a job doing something that he loved to do—sharing his passion and experience with others.

Captain Van Horn's Final Secret

If you want to increase your catch rate, two things are extremely important. You need to practice and learn to tie perfect knots that won't come loose under the pressure of a heavy fish. Secondly, keep your hooks sharp by having a sharpening tool handy and know how to use it. Never take your time on the water for granted, cherish every trip, and share your passion and experience with others. Take someone fishing who has never fished before.

Contact Information

Mosquito Coast Fishing Charters
Telephone: 1-866-790-8081
Cell phone: 407-416-1187
E-mail: captain@irl-fishing.com
Web site: www.irl-fishing.com

Capt. Blair Wiggins

Who says it doesn't take a rocket scientist to figure out fishing? Capt. Blair Wiggins grew up on Florida's Space Coast, and fishing has always been a part of his life. He attended the Cocoa Beach school system before enrolling in college and later enlisting in the Air Force. After the Air Force, he returned to the Space Coast and landed a job working on the space shuttle.

Blair's addiction to the water never left him, and when he returned to his old fishing grounds, all his spare time was consumed with the sport he loved. The urge to become a professional fishing guide soon won him over, and he bought a flats skiff to start his new career. He had been married several years and had a brand new baby boy when he made that fateful decision to quit his job and engage in charter fishing on a fulltime basis.

In a few years, he had developed his business to the point that he ran around 300 trips a year. His success and growing notoriety caught the attention of others, and he was asked to appear as the host-guide on several television shows. These experiences led him to realize what the next rung on his ladder of life would be.

Blair's charter business was named Addictive Fishing, and it was the perfect name for the television show he would start in 1999, along with his childhood friend, Kevin McCabe. Now he is content to do his television show and fish in tournaments. Blair fishes the

FLW tournament circuit and the Inshore Fishing Association with his son, Drayden.

Captain Wiggins's Final Secret

Patience and creativity are the two main secrets of fishing success. Simply put, have patience and never give up. Try new and creative presentations to get the fish to eat. Sometimes they just won't eat anything, but when they do, remember your presentation and how the fish responded to it, so you can duplicate it for similar conditions. The more successful presentations you can remember, the more fish you will catch, regardless of where you fish.

Contact Information

Blair Wiggins Enterprises/Addictive Fishing
Telephone: 321-631-8955
E-mail: blair@addictivefishing.com
Web site: addictivefishing.com

About the Art

Julie Sutton

I describe my style of painting watercolors as a form that breaks all the rules. Be that as it may, I still enjoy the process of painting that I have perfected over the years. I paint mostly with watercolors and have developed a technique that also includes pencil. I like detail in my painting, and using pencil, as artists would use in a portrait, enables me to achieve great detail and still have the ease and beauty of watercolor.

I have no plans to follow the rules of watercolor, and that is probably why my work is described as "something different." People tell me, "Don't change a thing," and I don't plan to.

Living in such a beautiful place as the Florida Keys and having the opportunity to fish regularly drives me to paint. Painting is like an addiction that needs to be fed regularly; otherwise, I feel like something in my life is missing. It is what gets me out of bed in the morning. When I am in-between paintings I am looking for an idea to feed the need.

Most of my paintings are borne from some fishing trip or some ride through the Everglades that inspired me to create. Instead of trying to save memories in photos I try to save them in paintings. My house is filled with paintings that are memories on canvas, tile, or paper.

Marine animals and wildlife will always be my favorite theme, and watercolors will always be my favorite form of painting. My portfolio has grown to include tropical birds and orchids, but I keep going back to the fish, the subject I love to paint the most.

Reproductions are available from Julie Sutton Marine Art
305-248-6126
www.juliesuttonmarineart.com

Index

Ron Presley is a retired professor of economics and a professional fishing guide. He is a licensed U.S. Coast Guard charter-boat captain and the secretary-treasurer of the Florida Guides Association.